50 Walks

INDUSTRIAL HERITAGE

D0300181

Produced by AA Publishing
© Automobile Association Developments Limited 2007
Illustrations © Automobile Association Developments Limited 2007

Published by AA Publishing (a trading name of Automobile
Association Developments Limited, whose registered office is Fanum
House, Basing View, Basingstoke, Hampshire RG21 4EA;
registered number 1878835)

 This product includes mapping data licensed
from Ordnance Survey® with the permission of
the Controller of Her Majesty's Stationery
Office. © Crown copyright 2007. All rights
reserved. Licence number 100021153

ISBN 978-0-7495-5552-8

A03033e

A CIP catalogue record for this book is available
from the British Library.

Some of the walks may appear in other AA publications.

Visit the AA Publishing website at www.theAA.com

Colour reproduction by Keene Group, Andover
Printed in China by Everbest Printing Company Ltd

Walking in Safety

All these walks are suitable for any reasonably fit person, but less experienced walkers should try the easier walks first. Route finding is usually straightforward, but you will find that an Ordnance Survey map is a useful addition to the route maps and descriptions.

Risks

Although each walk here has been researched with a view to minimising the risks to the walkers who follow its route, no walk in the countryside can be considered to be completely free from risk. Walking in the outdoors will always require a degree of common sense and judgement to ensure that it is as safe as possible.

- Be particularly careful on cliff paths and in upland terrain, where the consequences of a slip can be very serious.

- Remember to check tidal conditions before walking on the seashore.

- Some sections of route are by, or cross, busy roads. Take care and remember traffic is a danger even on minor country lanes.

- Be careful around farmyard machinery and livestock, especially if you have children with you.

- Be aware of the consequences of changes in the weather and check the forecast before you set out. Carry spare clothing and a torch if you are walking in the winter months. Remember the weather can change very quickly at any time of the year, and in moorland and heathland areas, mist and fog can make route finding much harder. Don't set out in these conditions unless you are confident of your navigation skills in poor visibility. In summer remember to take account of the heat and sun; wear a hat and carry spare water.

- On walks away from centres of population you should carry a whistle and survival bag. If you do have an accident requiring the emergency services, make a note of your position as accurately as possible and dial 999.

Legend & map

Legend

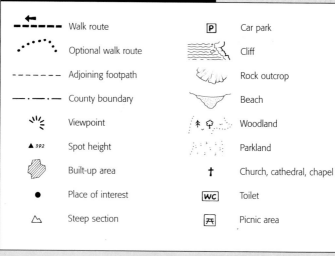

Walk route	P Car park
Optional walk route	Cliff
Adjoining footpath	Rock outcrop
County boundary	Beach
Viewpoint	Woodland
▲ 392 Spot height	Parkland
Built-up area	† Church, cathedral, chapel
● Place of interest	WC Toilet
△ Steep section	Picnic area

locator map

Contents

Contents

Rating: Each walk is rated for its relative difficulty compared to the other walks in this book. Walks marked 🚶🚶🚶 are likely to be shorter and easier with little total ascent. The hardest walks are marked 🚶🚶🚶.

Walking in Safety: For advice and safety tips see page 3.

Introduction

It was Queen Victoria's favourite politician, Benjamin Disraeli, who apparently first referred to England as 'the workshop of the world' in a speech to the House of Commons in 1838. Britain was then in the throes of one of the greatest peaceful revolutions ever witnessed, as the country transformed from what had been a largely agricultural nation into a fully-fledged industrial one.

The rusting remains of Britain's industrial heritage are unmatched throughout Europe, and can still be found throughout the country, as these 50 family-length walks will testify. They range from the mines and adits of the extractive industries which fed the furnaces and smelters to create the raw materials for manufacture, to the once-extensive network of railways and canals which transported them, and the factories, foundries, works and mills where the goods were finally produced.

At one time it was said that wherever you find a mine in the world, you'd find a Cornishman, often known as 'Cousin Jack.' Walk 2, from Redruth, follows the footsteps of generations of miners through Cornwall's tin-mining heartland, past Pednandrea Mine to the moorland 'cathedral' of Gwennap Pit, now the site of an interpretive centre. Another Tinners' Trail is followed from Pendeen on the Land's End peninsula, passing a number of former tin and copper mines at Geevor, Botallack and Carnyorth.

The green sheen of copper ore was the reason the Sygun Mines were sunk near the Snowdonian village of Beddgelert. This hard but rewarding 4-mile (6.4km) walk also takes you through the dramatic landscape of Cwm Bychan and the much-photographed Aberglaslyn Gorge.

The mineral sought for deep under the limestone of the Derbyshire White Peak was galena, or lead ore, and Walk 31 will take you through the delightful surroundings of Lathkill Dale, now part of a National Nature Reserve, but during the 18th and 19th centuries, a veritable hive of industry. This 5 mile (8km) stroll along the dale passes the ruins of Mandale Mine, a producer of lead for many years, and an important source of employment. Nature has largely healed the scars of industry now, and if you are there in early summer, you may get a sight of the delicate, bell-like purple-blue flowers of the nationally-rare Jacob's ladder.

Iron ore was the goal of the miners who worked the Rosedale Mines on the southern slopes of the North York Moors during the mid-19th century. The remains of the Rosedale East Mines, which opened in 1865, can be seen from Walk 42, and are still quite substantial. The long range of huge arches of the calcining kilns has an almost ecclesiastical air, like the cloisters of a long-lost cathedral. The 3½-mile (5.7km) walk from Thorgill can be extended to follow the line of the old railway which took the ore down from the moor by the steep 1-in-5 gradient of the Ingleby Incline.

The master of Victorian railway engineering was Isambard Kingdom Brunel, and you get a glimpse of one of his greatest achievements for the Great Western Railway on Walk 6 from Box in Wiltshire. When it was constructed in the mid-1800s, it was said to be the longest and steepest railway tunnel in the world. It ran for nearly two miles under Box Hill, with a gradient of 1 in 100, and used three million bricks to line the soft Cotswold oolitic limestone through which it was burrowed.

When we think of Blake's 'dark, Satanic mills' we usually think of the north of England, and the walks that visit the steel works of the Derwent Valley. Consett in Northumberland and Dunaskin across the border in Scotland would tend to bear that out.

But among the earliest places where iron was worked were in the water-powered blast funaces and hammer forges on Kentish Weald, as shown in Walk 11 from Brenchley.

And again, woollen, silk and cotton spinning mills are usually associated with Lancashire, but Walk 15 proves the lie with an easy walk around the north Essex market town of Halstead, where the Courtauld textile empire was founded by descendants of a Huguenot family in the early 19th century. Courtauld's white painted, weather-board fronted Townsford Mill finally closed in 1982, but at one time employed 1,400 women and young girls on 1,000 looms.

Using this Book

Information panels

A panel for each walk shows its relative difficulty, the distance and total amount of ascent. An indication of the gradients you will encounter is shown by the rating ▲▲▲ (no steep slopes) to **▲▲▲** (several very steep slopes).

Maps

Each of the 50 walks in this book has its own map, with the walk route clearly marked with a hatched line. Some can be extended by following an extra section of route marked with a dotted line, but for reasons of space, instructions for the extensions are not given in the text. The minimum time suggested for the walk is for reasonably fit walkers and doesn't allow for stops. Each walk has a suggested large-scale OS map which should be used in conjunction with the walk route map. Laminated aqua3 maps are longer lasting and water resistant.

Start Points

The start of each walk is given as a six-figure grid reference prefixed by two letters indicating which 100km square of the National Grid it refers to. You'll find more information on grid references on most Ordnance Survey maps.

Dogs

We have tried to give dog owners useful advice about how dog friendly each walk is. Please respect other countryside users. Keep your dog under control, especially around livestock, and obey local bylaws and other dog control notices.

Car Parking

Many of the car parks suggested are public, but occasionally you may find you have to park on the roadside or in a lay-by. Please be considerate when you leave your car, ensuring that access roads or gates are not blocked and that other vehicles can pass safely.

The Tinners' Trail at Pendeen

An absorbing walk through the historic tin and copper mining country of the Land's End Peninsula.

•DISTANCE•	5 miles (8km)
•MINIMUM TIME•	4hrs
•ASCENT / GRADIENT•	328ft (100m) ▲ ▲ ▲
•LEVEL OF DIFFICULTY•	🚶 🚶 🚶
•PATHS•	Coastal footpath, field paths and moorland tracks
•LANDSCAPE•	Spectacular coastal cliffs, old mining country and open moorland
•SUGGESTED MAP•	aqua3 OS Explorer 102 Land's End
•START / FINISH•	Grid reference: SW 383344
•DOG FRIENDLINESS•	Please keep dogs under control in field sections
•PARKING•	Free car park in centre of Pendeen village, opposite Boscaswell Stores, on the B3306
•PUBLIC TOILETS•	Pendeen car park and Geevor Tin Mine

BACKGROUND TO THE WALK

The tin and copper mines of Pendeen on the north coast of the Land's End Peninsula are redundant, as are all of Cornwall's mines; the culmination of the long decline of Cornish mining since its Victorian heyday. The deep mining of Cornwall lost out to cheap ore from surface strip mines in Asia and to the vagaries of the international market. At Pendeen the area's last working mine of Geevor closed in 1990 after years of uncertainty and false promise and despite vigorous efforts by the local community to save it. Today, the modern buildings of Geevor have been transformed into a fascinating mining museum, but it is the ruined granite chimney stacks and engine houses of the 19th-century industry that have given this mining coast its dramatic visual heritage. Below ground lies the true heritage of hard rock mining.

History and Character

To walk through this post-industrial rural landscape is to walk through a huge slice of Cornish history and character. Early in the walk you reach the Geevor Tin Mine and then the National Trust's Levant Engine House (see While You're There). From Levant the coast path runs on to Botallack, where the famous Crown's Mine Engine Houses stand on a spectacular shelf of rock above the Atlantic. The workings of the Crown's Mine ran out for almost 1 mile (1.6km) beneath the sea, and the mine was entered down an angled runway using wagons. You can visit the Crown's Mine Engine Houses by following a series of tracks down towards the sea from the route of the main walk. Flooding was a constant problem for these mines and some of the the earliest ever steam engines were developed to pump water from the workings. On the cliff top above the Crown's Mine the National Trust has restored the 19th-century façade of the Botallack Count House. This was the assaying and administrative centre for all the the surrounding mines.

Moorland Hills

From the Count House the way leads to the old mining villages of Botallack and Carnyorth, before climbing steadily inland to the exhilarating moorland hills of Carnyorth Common. This is the famously haunted landscape of Kenidjack Carn which local superstition identified as the playground of giants and devils. From the high ground the linear pattern of Pendeen's mining coast is spread out before you with the glittering Atlantic beyond. The walk then leads back towards Pendeen and past the Church of St John, built by the mining community in the 1850s from the hand-quarried rock of the hills above, yet another token of the remarkable skills of the Cornish hard rock miner.

Walk 1

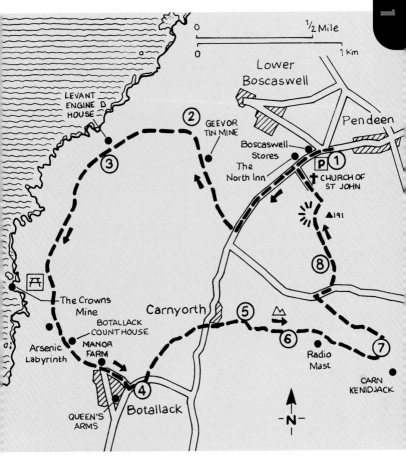

Walk 1 Directions

① Turn left out of the car park and follow the road to the entrance of the **Geevor Tin Mine**. Go down the drive to the reception building and keep to its left down a road between buildings, signposted '**Levant**'.

② Just beyond the buildings, turn left along a narrow path that soon bears right and becomes an unsurfaced track between walls. Turn left at a huge boulder and head towards a very tall chimney stack ahead. Continue across broken ground to the **Levant Engine House**.

Walk 1

> ### WHERE TO EAT AND DRINK   ⓘ
> Halfway along the route is the **Queen's Arms** in Botallack village, a traditional miners' pub that has retained much of its character. Pub meals are available. The **North Inn** at Pendeen is another traditional inn at the end of the walk and the **Geevor Museum** has a café.

③ Follow the bottom edge of Levant car park and then follow a rough track to reach the **Botallack Count House**. Keep on past **Manor Farm** and reach the public road at **Botallack**. Turn left, the **Queen's Arms** pub is straight down the road ahead.

④ Go left at the main road (watch for fast traffic) then turn left along **Cresswell Terrace** to a stile. Follow field paths to **Carnyorth**. Cross the main road, then follow the lane opposite, turning right at a junction, to reach a solitary house.

⑤ Keep left of the house, go over a stile and cross the field to the opposite hedge to reach a hidden stile. Follow a path through small fields towards a radio mast. Cross a final stile onto a rough track.

⑥ Go left, then immediately right at a junction. Keep on past the radio mast, then follow a path through gorse and heather to the rocky outcrop of **Carn Kenidjack**, (not always visible when misty).

> ### WHILE YOU'RE THERE   ⓘ
> A visit to the **Geevor Tin Mine** is worthwhile for the background to the history of Cornish mineral mining. Part of the experience is an underground tour and a visit to the old treatment sheds. The National Trust's restored engine house at **Levant Engine House** contains a remarkable reconstruction of a Cornish beam engine, the great driving force of every Victorian mine. The engine is regularly 'steamed up' to go through the stately rocking motion that powered deep water pumps and facilitated the movement of ore from below ground.

⑦ At a junction abreast of **Carn Kenidjack**, go back left along a path past a small granite parish boundary stone, eventually emerging on a road. Turn right and in about 140yds (128m), go left along an obvious broad track opposite a house.

⑧ Keep left at a junction. By two large stones on the left, bear off right along a grassy track. Go left over a big stone stile directly above the church and descend to the main road. Turn right to the **car park**.

> ### WHAT TO LOOK FOR   ⓘ
> Just below the track that runs past the Botallack Count House lie the ruins of an **arsenic labyrinth**. Mineral ore was often contaminated with arsenic. In the 19th century during times of low tin prices, this arsenic was collected by roasting ore in a calciner and passing the smoke through enclosed tunnels, the labyrinth. The cooling vapour deposited the arsenic on the labyrinth walls as a powder that was then exported, mainly to America as a pesticide against the boll weevil in the cotton fields. Its effect on both the labyrinth workers and cotton pickers does not bear thinking about.

Mines and Methodism at Redruth

A walk through Cornwall's mining heartland, visiting Methodism's famous outdoor 'cathedral' of Gwennap Pit along the way.

•DISTANCE•	4 miles (6.4km)
•MINIMUM TIME•	2hrs 30min
•ASCENT / GRADIENT•	442ft (135m) ▲ ▲ ▲
•LEVEL OF DIFFICULTY•	👫 👫 👫
•PATHS•	Field paths, rough tracks and surfaced lanes. Can be muddy after rain, 6 stiles
•LANDSCAPE•	Small fields and open heathland with quarry and mine remains
•SUGGESTED MAP•	aqua3 OS Explorer 104 Redruth & St Agnes
•START / FINISH•	Grid reference: SW 699421
•DOG FRIENDLINESS•	Dogs on lead through grazed areas
•PARKING•	Several car parks in Redruth
•PUBLIC TOILETS•	Redruth car parks. Gwennap Pit Visitor Centre, when open

BACKGROUND TO THE WALK

The old Cornish town of Redruth gained its name from mineral mining. In medieval times, the process of separating tin and copper from waste materials turned a local river blood-red with washed out iron oxide. The Cornish name for a nearby ford was Rhyd Druth, the 'ford of the red' and the village that grew around it became Redruth. The innovative engineering that developed in tandem with mining, turned Redruth and its adjoining town of Camborne into centres of Cornish industry.

Religious Zeal

Into the often bleak world of 18th-century mineral mining came the brothers John and Charles Wesley, their religious zeal as hot as a Redruth furnace. It's very appropriate that one of the most revered locations in Methodism is Gwennap Pit, near Redruth. Here the grassy hollow of a caved-in mine shaft was first used for secular gatherings and events, which included cock-fighting. But it wasn't long before the pit was commandeered as a sheltered venue for preaching. John Wesley preached here on 18 occasions between 1762 and 1789 and, in 1806, Gwennap Pit was transformed into the neat hollow of concentric turfed seating that you see today. Despite this 200 year legacy its freehold was not secured by the Methodist Church until 1978.

High Ground

The first part of this walk leads from the heart of Redruth past such significant mining relics as the great chimney stack of the Pednandrea Mine, just off Sea View Terrace. Once the stack towered eight storeys high; it's now reduced to four, but is still impressive. From here you soon climb to the high ground of Gwennap and Carn Marth. The field path that takes you to Gwennap Pit was once a 'highway' of people heading for this 'Cathedral of the moor'.

Today there is a Visitor Centre at the Pit, alongside the peaceful little Busveal Chapel of 1836.

From Gwennap Pit the walk leads onto the summit of Carn Marth and to one of the finest viewpoints in Cornwall; unexpectedly so because of the hill's modest profile. From above the flooded quarry on the summit you look north to the sea and to the hill of St Agnes Beacon. North east lies the St Austell clay country, south west is the rocky summit of Carn Brea with its distinctive granite cross; south east you can even see the cranes on Falmouth dockside. From the top of Carn Marth, the return route is all downhill along rough tracks and quiet country lanes that lead back to the heart of Redruth.

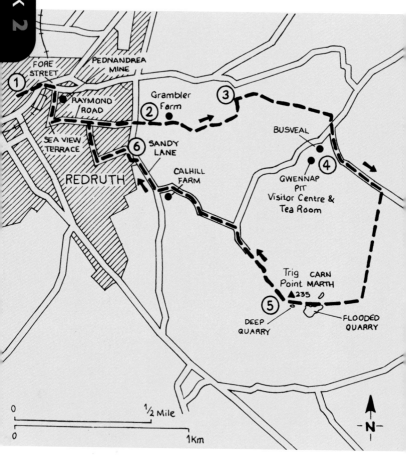

Walk 2 **Directions**

① From any of the car parks, make your way to **Fore Street**, the main street of Redruth. Walk up to a three-way junction (the railway station is down to the right) and take the middle branch, to the left of **Redruth Methodist Church**,

signposted '**To Victoria Park**'. This is **Wesley Street**. In just a few paces turn right on **Sea View Terrace**; the chimney stack of the **Pednandrea Mine** (see While You're There) is up to the left a few paces along the road. Pass **Basset Street** on the right and, where the streets cross, go left up **Raymond Road** to a T-junction with **Sandy Lane**.

② Cross the road with care, then follow the track opposite, signposted '**Public Bridleway**' and '**Grambler Farm**'. Go through a gate by the farm and continue to an open area. Bear left here and follow a much narrower track between hedges. When you reach a junction with another track turn left, signposted '**Gwennap Pit**'.

③ Go right, following the signposts for **Gwennap Pit**, cross a stile by a gate, then go through a small wooden gate. Keep ahead (there may be free-ranging pigs in the area so dogs should be kept under strict control). Go over a stile at the next gate and then follow the edge of the field ahead. Cross a final field towards a house and then walk down a lane past the house to a junction of surfaced roads at **Busveal**. Cross over and follow the road opposite for 100yds (91m) to **Gwennap Pit**.

> ### WHERE TO EAT AND DRINK ⓘ
> There is a small tea room at the **Gwennap Pit Visitor Centre**, which is open May–September, Monday–Friday 10–12:30 and 2–4:30; Saturday 10–12:30. You can picnic in Gwennap Pit itself, but please don't leave any litter. Redruth has several pleasant restaurants, cafés and pubs to choose from. Sample the wonderful local Cornish pasties from **WC Rowe's** in Fore Street. The **Red Lion** pub is also in Fore Street, and there is a fish and chip shop in Green Lane.

④ Follow the road away from **Gwennap Pit**. In about 300yds (274m) turn off to the right along a broad track, signposted '**Public Bridleway**'. Keep ahead at two crossings, then, at a final crossing beside a ruined building, turn right and follow a stony track up the hill to the prominent summit of **Carn Marth**.

> ### WHAT TO LOOK FOR ⓘ
> The field hedgerows throughout the walk are bright with wild flowers in spring and summer. Butterflies brighten the scene even more. Look for the handsome peacock butterfly (*Nymphalidae*), that feeds on the nectar of bramble flowers and also on the juice of berries. The brownish-red peacock is easily identified by the 'peacock-eye' markings on its hind wings.

⑤ Pass a flooded quarry (there's a viewpoint on the far side), then just beyond a trig point, bear round right on a path alongside the fenced-in rim of a deep quarry. On reaching a surfaced lane, turn left. Turn left at the next junction. Follow the lane to a T-junction with a road at **Calhill Farm**. Turn right and walk along **Sandy Road**, keeping a careful watch for traffic, for 275yds (251m).

⑥ Go left at a junction, signposted as a cycle route, and follow a lane right, then left into a broad avenue of houses. At a crossroads turn right along **Trefusis Road**. At the next junction turn left into **Raymond Road** and then right into **Sea View Terrace**. Turn left down **Wesley Street** and on into **Fore Street**.

> ### WHILE YOU'RE THERE ⓘ
> A visit to **Gwennap Pit** and its visitor centre is irresistible, but Redruth itself rewards exploration. Many buildings in Fore Street are Victorian Gothic and have some unusual features such as decorative brickwork. These, and the Italianate **Clock Tower** of 1828, reflect the boom period of Redruth's growth. The **Pednandrea Mine Chimney Stack**, passed early in the walk, was part of a mine that operated from about 1710 to 1891 producing copper, tin, lead and arsenic. The original height of the stack was between 126 and 140ft (38–43m).

Walk 3

Princetown: Thomas Tyrwhitt's Dream

There was great industrial activity here in the late 18th and early 19th centuries, but it's still the middle of nowhere!

•DISTANCE•	7 miles (11.3km)
•MINIMUM TIME•	3hrs
•ASCENT / GRADIENT•	328ft (100m) ▲ ▲ ▲
•LEVEL OF DIFFICULTY•	🏃 🏃 🏃
•PATHS•	Tracks, leat-side paths and rough moorland
•LANDSCAPE•	Open moorland
•SUGGESTED MAP•	aqua3 OS Outdoor Leisure 28 Dartmoor
•START / FINISH•	Grid reference: SX 588735
•DOG FRIENDLINESS•	Can be off the lead at all times, but watch for sheep
•PARKING•	Main car park in Princetown (honesty box)
•PUBLIC TOILETS•	By car park

BACKGROUND TO THE WALK

Even on a summer's day, when fluffy clouds scud across a blue sky and the high moor looks particularly lovely, Princetown is bleak. There's nothing soft and gentle about the place – most of the buildings are functional in the extreme, uncompromising, grey and harsh. The town, 1,395ft (425m) above sea level, and with an average annual rainfall of 82in (2,160mm), was founded by Sir Thomas Tyrwhitt in the late 18th century, and named in honour of the Prince Regent, to whom he was both a friend and private secretary.

Dartmoor Prison

Tyrwhitt persuaded the government to build a prison here for French prisoners from the Napoleonic wars. Building work started in 1806, and the first prisoners were in situ by 1809, joined by Americans in 1813. At one time 7,000 men were held. Closed in 1813, the prison reopened in 1850 as a civilian establishment, which it remains to this day – a monumental building, best seen from the Two Bridges to Tavistock road, to the north of the town.

There is mention of the ancient landmark of Nun's Cross (or Siward's Cross) as early as 1280, in documents concerning ownership of Buckland Abbey lands. Over 7ft (2.1m) high, it stands on the route of the Abbot's Way – between Buckfast Abbey and Tavistock – and marks the eastern boundary of Buckland Abbey lands. The word 'Siward' engraved on its eastern face may refer to the Earl of Northumberland who owned much land in this part of the country in Saxon times, or may indicate some connection to a family named Siward who lived nearby. 'Bocland' on the other face may be a reference to Buckland Abbey. The word 'Nun's' comes from the Celtic *nans*, meaning combe or valley.

The Devonport Leat is an amazing feat of engineering, carried out between 1793 and 1801 to improve water supplies to Devonport, now part of Plymouth, which at that time was being developed as a naval base. Originally 26½ miles (43km) long, it carried 2 million gallons (4.5 million litres) of water a day. Lined with granite slabs and conveying crystal-clear, fast-flowing water, today it provides an extremely attractive, level walking route through some otherwise fairly inhospitable terrain. The final part of the walk, back to Princetown, follows the abandoned railway track that Tyrwhitt planned to link Princetown with Plymouth. The line, the first iron railway in the county, opened in 1823. More of a tramway than a railway, the horse-drawn wagons carried coal and lime up from Plymouth, and took stone back. In 1881 commercial considerations caused the line to be taken over by the Princetown Railway Company. It reopened as a steam railway in 1883, until its eventual closure in 1956.

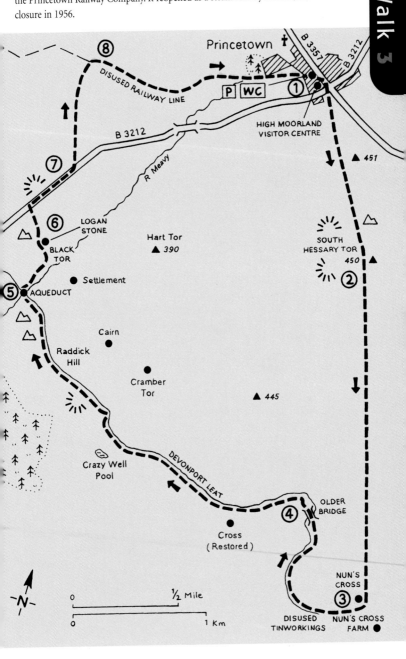

Walk 3

Walk 3 Directions

① Leave the car park past the toilets and turn right to pass the **High Moorland Visitor Centre**. Cross the road and follow the lane between the two pubs and their car parks behind. After 100yds (91m) a small gate leads to a broad gravelly track which ascends gently to **South Hessary Tor**, from which there are splendid views to **Plymouth Sound** ahead, and of the prison behind.

WHERE TO EAT AND DRINK ⓘ
The Plume of Feathers inn, originally a coaching house, is the oldest building in Princetown, dating from 1785. It has a campsite and camping barn and is a popular stopover for those exploring the moor on foot. Nearby is the Railway Inn. Both pubs are free houses, welcome families and serve good food.

---

② Follow the track as it drops down gently, passing boundary stones. It crosses two other tracks (look left for a view of the **Devonport Leat**) before dropping down to **Nun's Cross**. **Nun's Cross Farm** (originally a thatched house, *c* 1870) can be seen to the left.

③ Turn 90 degrees right at the cross to pick your way over a bumpy area of disused tin workings to find the end of the tunnel where the leat emerges. It's near the remains of a cottage under a beech and three hawthorn trees. Walk along the right bank of the leat.

④ Where the leat bends north cross it on **Older Bridge** (granite slabs) to walk along the left bank, with wonderful views of **Burrator reservoir** to the left. Follow the leat on; there are various crossing places and you should cross back to the right bank before descending to the valley of the **Meavy**; the leat picks up speed as it rushes downhill here, and the path is steep and rocky.

⑤ The Meavy is crossed via an aqueduct and the leat turns left. Take the grassy path right leading slightly uphill away from the river (there is a wealth of tin working evidence in the valley – worth an exploration). The path passes through a tumbledown granite wall; turn left and climb steeply up to **Black Tor**.

⑥ Go straight on past the **Logan Stone**, one of several on Dartmoor balanced in such a way that they can be rocked on their base, and on across open moorland to the road, with views of **Brentor**, **Swelltor Quarries** and the disused railway line ahead. Turn right at the road.

⑦ A few steps later, opposite the blocked off parking place, turn left and pick your way across tussocky grass, aiming for the mast on **North Hessary Tor**. This area is boggy in places, but passable.

⑧ At the railway track turn right and walk back to the edge of the town. The path splits, so keep left and through a small gate to join a tarmac road. Pass the **Devon Fire & Rescue Service** building to regain the car park on the right.

WHILE YOU'RE THERE ⓘ
Visit the High Moorland Visitor Centre (open 10AM–5PM), situated in the old Duchy Hotel, which you pass on Point ①. You'll find everything you ever wanted to know about the Dartmoor National Park here, and more besides. There's an information centre and shop, helpful staff, and a range of audio-visual and 'hands-on' displays.

From Wheddon Cross to Brendon's Heights

A sunken lane from Wheddon Cross leads up to Lype Hill, the high point of the Brendons.

•DISTANCE•	5¾ miles (9.2km)
•MINIMUM TIME•	3hrs
•ASCENT / GRADIENT•	850ft (260m) ▲▲▲
•LEVEL OF DIFFICULTY•	👥 👥 👥
•PATHS•	A rugged track, then little-used field bridleways, 4 stiles
•LANDSCAPE•	Rounded hills with steep, wooded sides
•SUGGESTED MAP•	aqua3 OS Outdoor Leisure 9 Exmoor
•START / FINISH•	Grid reference: SS 923387
•DOG FRIENDLINESS•	Mostly pasture, where dogs must be closely managed
•PARKING•	Village car park (free) on A396 at Wheddon Cross
•PUBLIC TOILETS•	At car park

BACKGROUND TO THE WALK

This walk takes in the highest point of the Brendons, Lype Hill, at 1,390ft (423m). The wrap-around view includes Dunkery Beacon, Wales and Dartmoor. The trig point itself stands on an ancient tumulus; the second apparent tumulus near by houses a modern-day water tank.

Brown Hill

Brendon means 'brown hill'. The shales and muddy sandstones are sea-bottom rocks: though the oldest in Somerset, they formed from the decomposition of still older mountains that have now completely disappeared. The Brendons are not particularly high, and are farmed to their tops, though the steeper sides are wooded. The scene appears timeless, but is actually rather recent: the hilltops were forested into the Middle Ages, and later became an industrial estate.

Return of the Iron Age

The Iron Age on Brendon saw the digging of long ramparts across the plateau, and a great settlement on the high ground. However, apart from a small fort at Elworthy Barrows, this activity wasn't in pre-Roman times, but in the more recent 19th century. A railway ran along the Brendon ridge from the iron ore mines. At its eastern end was a form of engineering we no longer see, except in Switzerland: a rope-assisted incline taking ore down to valley level. The ore then passed along the mineral railway to Watchet and the smelters of South Wales.

Below the mining areas and the farmland the hillsides have been less disturbed by man. Here, altitude, thin soils, and western levels of rainfall mean a sort of woodland more akin to the Scottish Highlands. You'll see the silver birch, for example – silver and gold if you're lucky enough to be here in late October. As well as a variety of autumn fungi in vivid colours, Hartcleeve has striking examples of Witch's Broom in its birch trees. These twig-clusters resemble untidy spherical nests but are in fact caused by a fungus infection (*ascomycete*) which interferes with the tree's growth hormones. A really well-established Witch's Broom can be 3ft (1m) across and will consist of hundreds of twigs.

The Sinking of Lanes

Putham Lane shows several centuries' worth of erosion in action: a speeded-up version of what's happening to the hills as a whole over millions of years (rather than a few hundred). Looking through the hedge you can see how much lower the lane is than the surrounding fields. Where the lane steepens, it also gets more deeply dug in; at its steepest point you can see bare grey bedrock in its floor. Where the track has dug itself down below the water table, a permanent stream trickles down it. After rain or during snowmelt this stream becomes a flood. Even at its low summer level, it's easy to see how it combines with feet (and, latterly, wheels) to excavate the track.

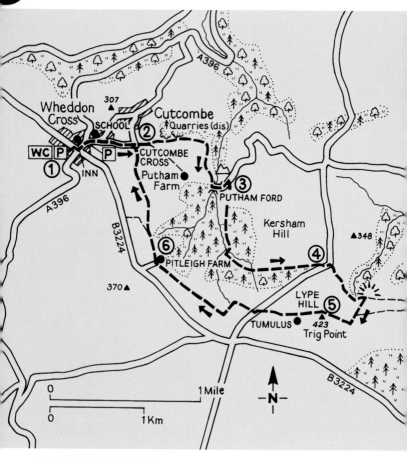

Walk 4 Directions

① From the main crossroads head towards Dunster, and bear right at the war memorial to pass a small car park on the right-hand side. After the school, bear right, following the signpost to **Puriton**. This is **Popery Lane** – and yes, the school we just passed was a Roman Catholic one. The sunken lane runs to **Cutcombe Cross**, where you keep ahead ('Luxburough via Putham Ford') then bear left at a sign into **Putham Lane**.

② Horses and tractors also use this narrow hedged track. At the bottom it crosses a ford, with a stone footbridge alongside. Now keep ahead on to a climbing lane surfaced with eroded tarmac.

WHERE TO EAT AND DRINK ⓘ
The **Rest And Be Thankful Inn** is beside the car park, and offers bar meals and real ales. Dogs can be accommodated in the downstairs dining area.

---

③ At the top of the steep climb a field gate on the right has an inconspicuous footpath signpost. It leads on to a green track that runs below and then into a wood. Watch out for a footpath sign and a stile beside a stream below. Cross the water and take a small path on its right, into an open space. A slightly wider path above slants up along a bracken clearing. After a stile it follows the foot of a wood, to join a forest road and then a tarred lane.

④ Turn left, down a wide verge, and take the upper of two gates on the right: the correct one has a stile and footpath sign. Head up the side of a wooded combe and across its top. Now a sea view is on the left, a stile and gate ahead. Don't cross,

---

WHILE YOU'RE THERE ⓘ
Bluebell woods are fairly common around Exmoor. However, a wood carpeted in snowdrops is more unusual. **Snowdrop Wood** at Wheddon Cross has caused traffic jams in the past and Exmoor National Park Authority now runs a park-and-ride scheme: this departs from the village car park during the February snowdrop season.

---

but turn right, and right again across the top of the field to a gate beside the trig point on **Lype Hill**.

⑤ Through the gate keep ahead across a field, with a tumulus 70yds (64m) away on the left, and after a gate bear left to follow the fence on the left to its corner. A gate ahead leads on to a road. Cross to a signposted gate, and bear left to the field's far corner. Turn left alongside a beech bank to a waymarked gate. Here turn right, with a fence on your right, and head down along field edges towards **Pitleigh Farm**. An awkward gate in deer fencing leads on to the driveway just to the left of the farm.

⑥ Cross the driveway into a green track. This becomes a fenced-in field edge to a deer-fence gate on the left. Turn right to continue as before with hedges now on your right. After two fields you reach a hedged track. This runs down to the crossroads in **Popery Lane**.

WHAT TO LOOK FOR ⓘ
Red, yellow and blue! In England the various **rights of way** are colour-coded. Through Highley Plantation you're on a footpath: look out for yellow paint-spots and waymarkers. Every gate after Lype Hill has the blue mark of a bridleway. Here there will be no stiles, but only gates, as horses can't climb stiles. At the start of the route, on Puriton Lane, a red mark shows the way through the wood. Here you are on a byway, in theory open to all traffic – although you are unlikely to meet a Rolls Royce coming the other way.

Bruton Combes

A walk around and above beautiful Bruton, a typical Somerset town, built in the early wealth of the wool industry.

•DISTANCE•	4½ miles (7.2km)
•MINIMUM TIME•	2hrs 15min
•ASCENT / GRADIENT•	500ft (150m) ▲▲▲
•LEVEL OF DIFFICULTY•	林林 林林 林林
•PATHS•	Enclosed tracks, open fields, an especially muddy farmyard
•LANDSCAPE•	Steep, grassy hills and combes
•SUGGESTED MAP•	aqua3 OS Explorer 142 Shepton Mallet
•START / FINISH•	Grid reference: ST 684348
•DOG FRIENDLINESS•	On leads or under close control
•PARKING•	Free parking off Silver Street, 50yds (46m) west of church; larger car park in Upper Backway
•PUBLIC TOILETS•	Near Church Bridge (walk start) and signposted from there

BACKGROUND TO THE WALK

Bruton is a typical Somerset town: originally Saxon but made prosperous by monks in the Middle Ages. The Augustinians moved in around 1150 and soon upgraded from priory to abbey. In the 10th century Bruton was the county's seventh largest town – though this was achieved with a tax-paying population of just 85!

Woolly Thinking

In the Middle Ages England was a one-product economy. The basic unit of wealth was the 346lb (160kg) woolsack. In 1310 some 35,000 of these were exported; in 1421, 75 per cent of all customs duties were paid on wool. In Parliament at London, the Lord Chancellor sat on a woolsack as a constant reminder of where his government's money came from. (Today it has been replaced by a wool-stuffed chair.)

As the price of raw wool started to fall, England turned to the manufacture of cloth, adding value to the product before it left the country. Bruton was ahead of the game here. Back in 1240 the town built its first fulling mill, sited on Quaperlake Street. Here the cloth was washed with fullers' earth, a form of clay that acts as a natural de-greasing compound. (Fuller's earth absorbs water as well as grease; it is responsible for the peculiarly sticky mud encountered on some of the walking country in this area.) The washed wool was then felted with water-powered hammers.

The raw wool market had been dominated by trading barons, who frequently became real aristocratic barons as a result. But the cloth trade saw, and to a great extent caused, the rise of the English middle class of clothiers and merchants. Their wool wealth rebuilt the church and a century later added its unusual second tower; they built the High Street and endowed the almshouses. Bruton clothiers traded with merchants in Hampshire, Dorset and London, and exported through the ports of Dorset. In the 1540s Bruton's fullers were importing woad (for dyeing) from the far Azores by way of Bristol. The Abbey saw its interests as parallel with those of the town, and subsidised the market cross and the licensing of fairs.

Wool Unspun

Mechanisation of the spinning and weaving processes was getting under way in the 1820s, but depression set in during the 1830s and Somerset never caught up with Lancashire. Hence Somerset wool villages remain non-industrial and pretty. Many medieval buildings survive behind the (fairly) modern shop signs and under the paintwork. Where others have collapsed through the ages, replacements have been inserted in the style of every century but always with sympathy. Today, competition from synthetic materials means the price of a fleece barely pays the wages of the man who shears it. In Bruton you'll see the evidence of wool wealth on every side. The one thing you probably won't see is a sheep.

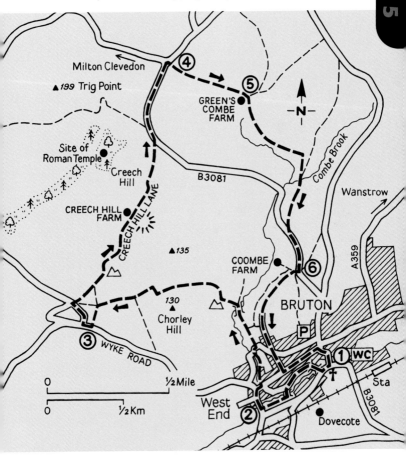

Walk 5 Directions

① With the church on your left and the bridge on your right, head down **Silver Street** for 30yds (27m) to a small car park in **Coombe Street**. The old packhorse bridge over the **River Brue** leads into

Lower Backway. Turn left for 350yds (320m), ignoring an arch leading towards a footbridge but then taking a path between railed fences to a second footbridge. Turn right along the river to **West End**.

② Turn right over the river and right again into the end of **High**

Street, but at once turn off uphill on to a walled path called **Mill Dam**. At the lane above turn right along a track signed 'Huish Lane'. Just after a footbridge fork left: the hedged track is fairly steep and muddy, bending right then left to a lane (**Wyke Road**).

③ Turn right for a few steps, then right again, and after 220yds (201m) turn right past farm buildings on to an uphill track, **Creech Hill Lane**. This becomes a hedged tunnel, then emerges at **Creech Hill Farm**. This may be one of the county's less tidy farms, but boasts one of its finest views. Pass along the front of the farm and out to the **B3081**. Turn left over the hill crest to a triangular junction.

④ Turn right for 40yds (37m) to a public bridleway sign and a gate on the right. Go straight down the combe below; at its foot keep to the left of **Green's Combe Farm** and above an intermittent wall, to turn down through a gate between the farm buildings.

⑤ Continue down the farm's access track for ¼ mile (400m) until it bends right. Here keep ahead through a field gate with a blue waymarker, on to a green track. After 200yds (183m), beside three stumps, turn downhill, to the left of a row of hazels, to a gate. Pass through a small wood to a gate and waymarked track. When this emerges into open field follow the fence above to join the **B3081**. Turn left, uphill, to the entrance to **Coombe Farm**.

⑥ Ignoring a stile on the left, go through an ivy-covered wall gap, then down the driveway for barely a dozen paces before turning left on to a wide path under sycamore trees. The path rises gently, with a bank on its left. On reaching open grassland, keep to the left edge to find a descending path that becomes **St Catherine's Lane**. Weavers' cottages are on the right as the street descends steeply into **Bruton**. Turn left along the **High Street**. At its end turn right down **Patwell Street** to **Church Bridge**.

Brunel's Great Tunnel Through Box Hill

A hilly walk around Box Hill, famous for its stone and Brunel's greatest engineering achievement.

•DISTANCE•	3¼ miles (5.3km)
•MINIMUM TIME•	1hr 45min
•ASCENT / GRADIENT•	508ft (155m) ▲▲▲
•LEVEL OF DIFFICULTY•	梵 梵 梵
•PATHS•	Field and woodland paths, bridle paths, metalled lanes, 15 stiles
•LANDSCAPE•	River valley and wooded hillsides
•SUGGESTED MAP•	aqua3 OS Explorer 156 Chippenham & Bradford-on-Avon
•START / FINISH•	Grid reference: ST 823686
•DOG FRIENDLINESS•	Can be off lead on Box Hill Common and in woodland
•PARKING•	Village car park near Selwyn Hall
•PUBLIC TOILETS•	Opposite Queens Head in Box

BACKGROUND TO THE WALK

Box is a large straggling village that sits astride the busy A4 in hilly country halfway between Bath and Chippenham. Although stone has been quarried here since the 9th century, Box really found fame during the 18th-century when the local stone was used for Bath's magnificent buildings. The construction of Box Tunnel also uncovered immense deposits of good stone and by 1900 Box stone quarries were among the most productive in the world, employing over 700 men. Little trace can be seen above ground today, except for some fine stone-built houses in the village and a few reminders of the industry on Box Hill.

Appointed Engineer

In 1833, the newly created Great Western Railway appointed Isambard Kingdom Brunel (1806–59) as engineer. His task was to build a railway covering the 118 miles (190km) from London to Bristol. The problems and projects he encountered on the way would help to make him the most famous engineer of the Victorian age. After a relatively straightforward and level start through the Home Counties, which earned the nickname 'Brunel's Billiard Table', he came to the hilly Cotswolds. (Incidentally, the Provost of Eton thought the line would be injurious to the discipline of the school and the morals of the pupils.)

Brunel's Famous Tunnel

The solution at Box would be a tunnel, and at nearly 2 miles (3.2km) long and with a gradient of 1:100 it would be the longest and steepest in the world at the time. It would also be very wide. Already controversial, Brunel ignored the gauge of other companies, preferring the 7ft (2.1m) used by tramways and roads (and, it was believed, Roman chariots). He also made the tunnel dead straight, and, never one to 'hide his light', the alignment was calculated so the dawn sun would shine through on his birthday on 9th April. Unfortunately he did not allow for atmospheric refraction and was two days out!

Passage to Narnia?

All was on a grand scale: a ton of gunpowder and candles was used every week, 3 million bricks were fired to line the soft Cotswold limestone and 100 navvies lost their lives working on the tunnel. After 2½ years the way was open, and although Brunel would ultimately lose the battle of the gauges, his magnificent line meant that Bristol was then a mere two hours from the capital. Although artificial, like many large dark holes, the tunnel has collected its fair share of mystery with tales of noises, people under the hill and trains entering the tunnel, never to re-emerge. But as is often the case, the explanations are rather more mundane. To test excavation conditions, Brunel dug a small trial section alongside what is now the eastern entrance and the military commandeered this section during World War Two as a safe and fairly secret store for ammunition, records and top brass. Sadly it is not a passage to Narnia!

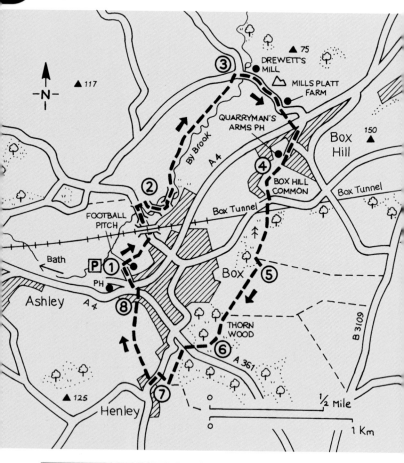

Walk 6 **Directions**

① Facing the **recreation ground**, walk to the left-hand side of the football pitch to join a track in the corner close to the railway line. When you reach the lane, turn left, pass beneath the railway, cross a bridge and take the arrowed footpath, to the right, before the second bridge.

② Walk beside the river, cross a footbridge and turn right. Cross a further footbridge and continue to a stile. Walk through water-meadows close to the river, go through a squeeze stile and maintain direction. Shortly, bear left to a squeeze stile in the field corner. Follow the right-hand field edge to a stile and lane.

③ Turn right, then right again at the junction. Cross the river, pass **Drewett's Mill** and steeply ascend the lane. Just past **Mills Platt Farm**, take the arrowed footpath ahead across a stile. Continue steeply uphill to a stile and cross the A4. Ascend steps to a lane and proceed straight on up **Barnetts Hill**. Keep right at the fork, then right again and pass the **Quarryman's Arms**.

④ Keep left at the fork and continue beside **Box Hill Common** to a junction. Take the path straight ahead into woodland. Almost

immediately, fork left and follow the path close to the woodland edge. As it curves right into the beech wood, bear left and follow the path through the gap in the wall and then immediately right at the junction of paths.

⑤ Follow the bridle path to a fork. Keep left, then turn right at the T-junction and take the path left to a stile. Cross a further stile and descend into **Thorn Wood**, following the stepped path to a stile at the bottom.

⑥ Continue through scrub to a stile and turn right beside the fence to a wall stile. Bear right to a further stile, then bear left uphill to a stile and the **A361**. Cross over and follow the drive ahead. Where it curves left by stables, keep ahead along the arrowed path to a house. Bear right up the garden steps to the drive and continue uphill to a T-junction.

⑦ Turn left, then on entering **Henley**, take the path right, across a stile. Follow the field edge to a stile and descend to an allotment and stile. Continue to a stile and gate.

⑧ Follow the drive ahead, bear left at the garage and take the metalled path right, into **Box**. Cross the main road and continue to the **A4**. Turn right, then left down the access road back to **Selwyn Hall**.

The Swanage Eccentric

The peculiar story of a coastal town that not only exported stone but imported it too.

•DISTANCE•	4¼ miles (6.8km)
•MINIMUM TIME•	3hrs
•ASCENT / GRADIENT•	509ft (155m) ▲▲▲
•LEVEL OF DIFFICULTY•	🏃 🏃 🏃
•PATHS•	Grassy paths, rocky tracks, pavements, 4 stiles
•LANDSCAPE•	Spectacular cliff scenery, undulating hills, Swanage town
•SUGGESTED MAP•	aqua3 OS Explorer OL 15 Purbeck & South Dorset
•START / FINISH•	Grid reference: SZ 031773
•DOG FRIENDLINESS•	Some town walking
•PARKING•	Durlston Country Park (charge)
•PUBLIC TOILETS•	Durlston Country Park; behind Heritage Centre on harbour (small charge); Peveril Point

BACKGROUND TO THE WALK

In the early 19th century Swanage was a small, bustling, industrial port that shipped stone from the 60 or so quarries in the area. A growing fashion for seabathing would, in time, change the focus of the town for ever. The real changes to the face of Swanage came, however, with the extraordinary collecting habit of one George Burt, a contractor with an eye for fancy architecture.

Instant Architecture

With his uncle, John Mowlem, a local stonemason and philanthropist, Burt shipped marble from the quarries of Purbeck to London, where old buildings were being knocked down to make way for a new wave of construction. Reluctant to see such splendid stonework discarded, Burt salvaged whole pieces, transported them back in the company ships as ballast, and re-erected them in his home town, giving Swanage an unexpected, instant architectural heritage.

The first influence you see of this man is as you walk past the Town Hall. Burt had donated a reasonably plain and simple building to the town in 1872, but in 1883 he added a façade by Sir Christopher Wren, appropriately in Portland stone, which he had rescued from the front of the Mercers' Hall in London's Cheapside. Architectural commentator Sir Nikolaus Pevsner described its florid carvings of stone fruit and wreaths as 'overwhelmingly undisciplined'. Next, in the park near the pier, are a grand archway removed from Hyde Park Corner, three statues and some columns rescued from Billingsgate Market. There's also an absurd but rather elegant clock tower, removed from the south end of London Bridge in 1867, where it had been set as a memorial to the Duke of Wellington.

Burt's Folly

Durlston Castle is an original folly by Burt dating from 1887, designed from the start as a clifftop restaurant on Durlston Head. It has an unexpected educational element, as useful facts and figures from around the world are carved into great stone slabs set into the walls below – for example, in terms of sunshine, the 'longest day' in London is 16½ hours, while in Spitzbergen it is 3½ months. Burt added a large, segmented stone globe of the world but it's rather grey and a little disappointing.

Railway Revival

George Burt was also influential in bringing the railway to Swanage in 1885 – this gave major impetus to the development of the town as a thriving seaside resort. The railway fell under the Beeching axe in the early 1960s, but was revived by enthusiasts who, early in 2002, at last achieved their ambition of linking back up to the main line station at Wareham. Today the mournful 'poop' of its steam train's whistle can be heard across the Isle of Purbeck as it transports visitors on a nostalgic trip between Swanage and Corfe Castle.

Walk 7

Walk 7 Directions

① Take the footpath directly below the visitor centre car park, signed to the lighthouse. Steps lead down through some trees. With the sea ahead, follow the path round to the right, joining the coastal path. Keep right, towards the lighthouse, down the steep path. As you climb up the other side, look back and down to admire the spectacular **Tilly Whim Caves** cut into the ledges of the

Walk 7

cliff. Pass the **lighthouse** and turn right, then go through a kissing gate to follow the path with butterfly markers up the steep side of **Round Down**, with views to St Adhelm's Head.

② At the top bear right, heading inland and parallel with a wall. Go down a slope, through a gate and across a footbridge, then turn up to the right. At a wooden gate turn left over a stone stile, following the butterfly marker. After another stile you can see the roll of the Purbeck Hills ahead and the roofs of Swanage to the right. Cross a stile and go down a broad, grassy track. Beyond a stile by a farm this track narrows and begins to climb steeply. Continue straight ahead on to the road and follow this into the town, with the prominent **church** in front of you.

WHERE TO EAT AND DRINK ⓘ
You can get a meal at the Durlston Castle restaurant, which will also supply you with tea (or something stronger), and ice cream. For my money, however, you can't beat fish and chips eaten down on the harbour, shared with the seagulls and watching the activity in the bay.

---

③ Turn right on to the main road. It's worth pausing to admire the little square with its butter cross and old stone houses tumbling down to the church. Continue along the street, but look out for: the modest metal plaque above the front door of **No 82A**, home of Taffy Evans; the elaborate **Wesley memorial**; and the extraordinary **Town Hall** with its Wren frontage.

④ At the square bear left beside the **Heritage Centre**, towards the harbour. Turn right and pass the entrance to the pier. Keep left at the

---

WHILE YOU'RE THERE ⓘ
Pop into Studland Heritage Centre (closed in winter) and learn more about the area, including tales of smuggling and the development of Purbeck's stone quarrying industry. Pay a nominal fee and enjoy the delights of Swanage's Victorian pier, which has penny-in-the-slot machines and 'Wot the butler saw' – no seaside visit can be complete without it. The pier suffered in the past from neglect and threat of demolition, but is undergoing restoration.

---

yellow marker, then bear right, up the hill, past a modern apartment block and a bizarre stone tower, to reach the tip of **Peveril Point**, with its coastguard station.

⑤ Turn right and walk up the grassy slope along the top of the cliffs. Take the path in the top corner and follow the Victoria's head markers to a road. Turn left through an area of pleasant Victorian villas. Erosion of the coastal path means a well-signed detour here, along the street, down to the left and left into woodland, signposted to the lighthouse. Follow the path for about ½ mile (800m) along the cliff top to **Durlston Head**. Pass **Durlston Castle** on your left and turn down to examine Burt's great stone globe. Stagger back up the steep hill to return to the car park.

WHAT TO LOOK FOR ⓘ
On the High Street, the small terraced house at No 82A bears a modest metal plaque above the front door, announcing that this was the home of Petty Officer Edgar 'Taffy' Evans. An experienced seaman, he was described by a companion as 'a giant worker'. He perished with Captain Scott from the effects of frostbite and exhaustion on the way back from the South Pole in 1912.

Bursledon and Boatbuilding

Exploring both sides of the yacht-filled Hamble estuary.

•**DISTANCE**•	6 miles (9.7km)
•**MINIMUM TIME**•	3hrs
•**ASCENT / GRADIENT**•	164ft (50m) ▲ ▲ ▲
•**LEVEL OF DIFFICULTY**•	🚶 🚶 🚶
•**PATHS**•	Riverside, field and woodland paths, some stretches of road
•**LANDSCAPE**•	River estuary, farmland dotted with patches of woodland
•**SUGGESTED MAP**•	aqua3 OS Outdoor Leisure 22 New Forest
•**START / FINISH**•	Grid reference: SU 485067
•**DOG FRIENDLINESS**•	Keep dogs on lead
•**PARKING**•	Pay-and-display car park by Quay in Hamble
•**PUBLIC TOILETS**•	Hamble

BACKGROUND TO THE WALK

The tidal Hamble estuary between Bursledon and the Southampton Water is not only one of the longest in the county, it's also one of Britain's busiest. The river has a long history of human activity from the first Saxon settlers, who used it as a route to the fertile areas inland, to its current status as Britain's premier yachting centre. Today, this stretch of river is filled with yachts and pleasure craft, but between the 14th and the early 19th century both Hamble-le-Rice (its formal name) and Bursledon were major centres for naval shipbuilding.

Great Shipbuilders

The valley provided a rich supply of timber for the wooden warships, the ironworks at nearby Hungerford Bottom supplied essential fastenings and the bend in the river at Bursledon offered the necessary shelter for the Hamble to be ideal for this vital industry. At its peak during the Napoleonic Wars the Elephant Yard, next to the Jolly Sailor pub, built the 74-gun HMS *Elephant*, Nelson's flagship at the Battle of Copenhagen. Two great local shipbuilders were George Parsons, who built the *Elephant*, and Philemon Ewer, who died in 1750 and whose epitaph states 'during the late war with France and Spain built seven large ships of war'. The best known ship to be built at Hamble was the *Grace Dieu* for Henry V in the 15th century. It was at Hamble Common in 1545 that Henry VIII watched in horror as his famous flagship, the 91-gun *Mary Rose*, sank with the loss of 700 men just off the coast.

The six tiny Victory Cottages you pass in Lower Swanwick, just a stone's throw from the present-day Moody's yard, were built in the late 18th century to house shipyard workers during the Napoleonic Wars. The bustling marinas and yacht moorings at Bursledon, best viewed from the terrace of the Jolly Sailor, have only appeared in the last 70 years.

Today, the villages of Hamble and Old Bursledon are a delight to explore. Hamble has a twisting main street, lined with pretty Georgian buildings, leading down to the Quay with lovely river views. Old Bursledon has a High Street but no shops, just peaceful lanes dotted with interesting buildings, in particular the timber-framed Dolphin, a former pub, with a 16th-century porch. Tucked away on the slopes above the river and scattered along lanes leading nowhere, you'll find it a pleasure to stroll through, especially if you pause at the Hacketts Marsh viewpoint where a well-placed bench affords the chance to admire the view.

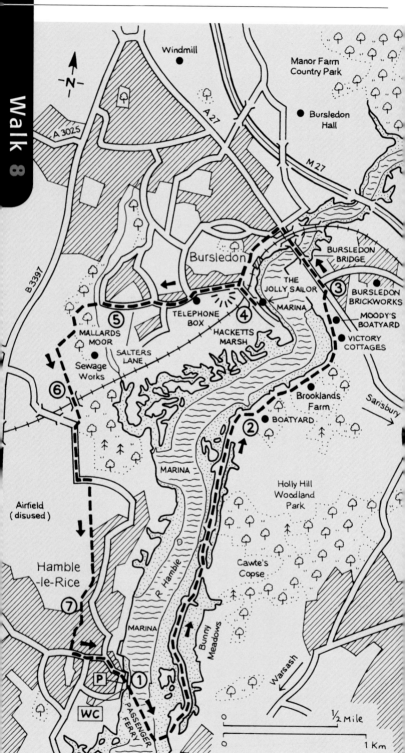

Windmill

Manor Farm
Country Park

● Bursledon
Hall

A 27

M 27

A 3025

B 3397

Bursledon

BURSLEDON
BRIDGE

THE
JOLLY SAILOR

⑤

TELEPHONE
BOX

④

MARINA

③

BURSLEDON
BRICKWORKS

MOODY'S
BOATYARD

VICTORY
COTTAGES

MALLARDS
MOOR

HACKETTS
MARSH

SALTERS
LANE

Sewage
Works

⑥

Brooklands
Farm

② BOATYARD

Sarisbury →

MARINA

Holly Hill
Woodland
Park

Airfield
(disused)

Cawte's
Copse

Hamble
-le-Rice

R. Hamble

⑦

MARINA

Bunny
Meadows

Warsash

①

P

WC

PASSENGER FERRY

½ Mile

1 Km

Walk 8 Directions

① From the quayside car park, walk to the pontoon and take the passenger ferry across the estuary to **Warsash** (weather permitting Monday–Friday 7AM–5PM; Saturday, Sunday 9AM–6PM). Turn left along the raised gravel path beside the estuary and mudflats. Cross a footbridge and continue to a gravelled parking area. During exceptionally high tides the path may flood, so walk through the car park and rejoin it by the marina.

> **WHERE TO EAT AND DRINK** ⓘ
> There's a range of pubs and tea rooms in Hamble, notably the **Compass Point Café**, **Village Tea Rooms** and the **Bugle**. Stop off at the **Jolly Sailor** in Bursledon for good ale and fine river views, or the quieter **Vine** in Old Bursledon.

② At a boatyard, keep right of a boat shed. Bear left beyond, between the shed and **TS Marina**, and bear right in front of the **Sales Office** to rejoin the path. Reach a lane, turn left and pass **Victory Cottages** on your right. Continue by **Moody's Boatyard** to the A27.

③ Turn left and cross **Bursledon Bridge**. (Turn right before the bridge to visit **Bursledon Brickworks**). Pass beneath the railway and turn left, signed to 'the Station'. Turn left into **Station Road**, then left again into the station car park, following signs for

> **WHAT TO LOOK FOR** ⓘ
> Just before high tide you may see up to 12 species of **waders**, including dunlin, redshank, lapwing and curlew, and wildfowl – shelduck, teal and Brent geese (in winter) – feeding on the rich mudflats as you stroll the riverside path.

the **Jolly Sailor**. Climb a steep path to the road. Turn left at the junction, then left again to reach the pub.

④ Return along the lane and fork left along the **High Street** into **Old Bursledon**. Pause at the excellent viewpoint at **Hacketts Marsh**, then bear left at the telephone box along the **High Street**. Pass the **Vine Inn** and **Salterns Lane**, then at a right bend, bear off left by **Thatched Cottage** along a footpath.

⑤ Join a metalled lane beside the drive to the **Coach House** then, as the lane curves left, keep ahead beside a house called **Woodlands**, following the path downhill to a stream. Proceed uphill through woodland (**Mallards Moor**). At a junction of paths on the woodland fringe, bear left with the bridleway, then at a concrete road bear right, then left to join a fenced path.

> **WHILE YOU'RE THERE** ⓘ
> Visit **Bursledon Brickworks**. Restored by a trust in 1990, it is the last surviving example of a steam-driven brickworks in the country, with a working steam engine, exhibition on the history and development of brickmaking, hands-on activities and special events.

⑥ Cross a railway bridge and soon pass a barrier to a road. Keep left round a sharp left-hand bend. Look out for a waymarked footpath on your right and follow this path behind houses for ½ mile (800m).

⑦ Join a metalled path and proceed past modern housing to a road. Follow this out to **Hamble Lane** and turn left to join the **High Street**. At the roundabout, bear right down **Lower High Street** back to the **Quay** and car park.

West Itchenor – Harbour Sails and Trails

Chichester Harbour's plentiful wildlife and colourful yachting activity form the backdrop to this fascinating waterside walk.

•DISTANCE•	3½ miles (5.7km)
•MINIMUM TIME•	1hr 30min
•ASCENT / GRADIENT•	Negligible
•LEVEL OF DIFFICULTY•	
•PATHS•	Shoreline, field tracks and paths, 1 stile
•LANDSCAPE•	Open farmland and coastal scenery
•SUGGESTED MAP•	aqua3 OS Explorer 120 Chichester, South Harting & Selsey
•START / FINISH•	Grid reference: SZ 797013
•DOG FRIENDLINESS•	Waterside paths are ideal for dogs but keep under control on stretches of open farmland and on short section of road. Dogs permitted on harbour water tour
•PARKING•	Large pay-and-display car park in West Itchenor
•PUBLIC TOILETS•	West Itchenor

BACKGROUND TO THE WALK

Weekend sailors flock to Chichester's vast natural harbour, making it one of the most popular attractions on the south coast. The harbour has about 50 miles (81km) of shoreline and 17 miles (28km) of navigable channel, though there is almost no commercial traffic. The Romans cast an approving eye over this impressive stretch of water and established a military base and harbour at nearby Fishbourne after the Claudian invasion of Britain in AD 43. Charles II had a fondness for the area too and kept a yacht here.

Boat Building Legacy

Situated at the confluence of the Bosham and Chichester channels of the estuary is the sailing village of Itchenor, with its main street of picturesque houses and cottages running down to the waterfront. Originally named Icenor, this small settlement started life as a remote, sparsely populated community, but by the 18th century it had begun to play a vital role in the shipbuilding industry. Small warships were built here by the merchants of Chichester, though in later years shipbuilding ceased altogether and any trace of its previous prosperity disappeared beneath the houses and the harbour mud. However, the modern age of leisure and recreation has seen a revival in boat building and yachting and today Itchenor is once again bustling with boat yards, sailors and chandlers.

Important Tidal Habitat

But there is much more to Chichester Harbour than sailing. Take a stroll along the harbour edge and you will find there is much to capture the attention. With its inter-tidal habitats, the harbour is a haven for plant life and wildlife. Wading birds such as curlew, redshank and dunlin can be seen using their differently shaped bills to extract food from the ecologically rich mudflats and terns may be spotted plunging to catch fish. Plants include sea lavender and glasswort and many of them are able to resist flooding and changing saltiness. Salt marsh is one of the typical habitats of Chichester Harbour and the plants which make up the marsh grow in different places according to how often they are flooded.

Stand on the hard at West Itchenor and you can look across the water towards neighbouring Bosham, pronounced 'Bozzum'. Better still, take the ferry over there and explore the delights of this picturesque harbour village. It was from here that Harold left for Normandy before the Norman Conquest of 1066. 'The sea creek, the green field, the grey church,' wrote Tennyson and this sums up perfectly the charm of this unspoilt corner of Sussex. Take a little time to have a look at the Church of the Holy Trinity and its Saxon tower base while you're there.

Walk 9

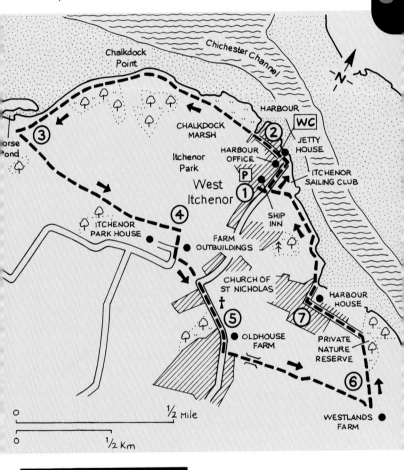

<img_1 map showing Chichester Channel, Chalkdock Point, Chalkdock Marsh, Itchenor Park, West Itchenor, Harbour Office, Jetty House, Itchenor Sailing Club, Ship Inn, Itchenor Park House, Farm Outbuildings, Church of St Nicholas, Oldhouse Farm, Harbour House, Private Nature Reserve, Westlands Farm, Horse Pond. Scale: ½ Mile, ½ Km. Numbered points 1–7.>

Walk 9 Directions

① From the car park walk along to the road and bear left, heading towards the harbour front. Pass the **Ship Inn** and make your way down to the water's edge. Look for the harbour office and the toilets and follow the footpath to the left of **Jetty House**.

② Cut between hedging and fencing to reach a boat yard and then continue ahead on the clear

---

WHERE TO EAT AND DRINK ⓘ
The **Ship Inn** at West Itchenor dates back to 1803 and was largely rebuilt after a fire in the 1930s. The spacious interior fills up on summer weekends, but there is a good choice of food. The **Chichester Harbour boat trip** offers light refreshments and is licensed for drinks.

---

country path. Keep left at the next junction and shortly the path breaks cover to run hard by the harbour and its expanses of mud flats. Cross **Chalkdock Marsh** and continue on the waterside path.

③ Keep going until you reach a footpath sign. Turn left here by a sturdy old oak tree and follow the path away from the harbour edge, keeping to the right-hand boundary of the field. Cross a stile to join a track on a bend and continue ahead, still maintaining the same direction. Pass **Itchenor Park House** on the right and approach some farm outbuildings.

④ Turn right by a brick and flint farm outbuilding and follow the path, soon merging with a concrete track. Walk ahead to the next junction and turn left by a white gate, down to the road. Bear right here, pass the speed restriction sign and soon you reach the little **Church of St Nicholas**.

WHILE YOU'RE THERE ⓘ
Enjoy a **water tour of Chichester Harbour** during the summer months, or go in winter when there are regular trips for bird watching, accompanied by an expert guide. These tours enable you to appreciate the harbour's treasures at first hand and you can see at close quarters some of the many vessels that use it. There are about 12,000 resident boats, with many visiting yachts from the USA, the Far East and Europe.

---

⑤ Follow the road along to **Oldhouse Farm** and then turn left at the footpath sign to cross a footbridge. Keep to the right of several barns and follow the path straight ahead across the field. Pass a line of trees and keep alongside a ditch on the right into the next field. The path follows the hedge line, making for the field corner. Ahead are the buildings of **Westlands Farm**.

⑥ Turn sharp left by the footpath sign and follow the path across the field. Skirt the woodland, part of a private nature reserve, and veer left at the entrance to **the Spinney**. Follow the residential drive to **Harbour House**.

WHAT TO LOOK FOR ⓘ
Over half way round the walk you pass the delightful 13th-century **Church of St Nicholas**, dedicated to the patron saint of children and seafarers. The little church, which has a lychgate, is usually open and inside there are some fascinating treasures. Changes in the window arrangements were made in the 14th century to provide additional light and there have been a number of alterations and additions over the years.

---

⑦ Turn right just beyond it and follow the path along the edge of the harbour. Keep going along here until you reach **Itchenor Sailing Club**. Bear left and walk up the drive to the road. Opposite you should be the **Ship Inn**. Turn left to return to the car park.

Alfold and the Lost Canal

Take a walk through the wildwoods along a derelict canal tow path.

•DISTANCE•	4¾ miles (7.7km)
•MINIMUM TIME•	2hrs
•ASCENT / GRADIENT•	164ft (50m) ▲ ▲ ▲
•LEVEL OF DIFFICULTY•	🚶 🚶 🚶
•PATHS•	Old canal tow path, field and forest paths. muddy after rain
•LANDSCAPE•	Mainly wooded countryside, some views across farmland
•SUGGESTED MAP•	aqua3 OS Explorer 134 Crawley & Horsham
•START / FINISH•	Grid reference: TQ 026350
•DOG FRIENDLINESS•	On lead in Sidney Wood and Oakhurst Farm
•PARKING•	Forestry Commission car park between Alfold and Dunsfold
•PUBLIC TOILETS•	None on route

BACKGROUND TO THE WALK

As you amble through the depths of Sidney Wood along the sinuous tow path of the long abandoned Wey and Arun canal, you can hardly fail to ponder the significance of this overgrown, muddy trench. In the closing years of the 18th century the Industrial Revolution was in full swing. The roads, such as they were, could simply not cope with carrying coal, heavy raw materials and finished goods over long distances. But in southern England, there was an even more urgent imperative. France was in turmoil and the dawn of a new century found Britain engaged in the Napoleonic Wars. Coastal cargoes in the English Channel were at risk and a new route was needed between London and the South Coast.

Building the Link

River traffic had flowed between London and Guildford since 1653, and the River Arun had been navigable to Pallingham Quay, near Pulborough, since Elizabethan times. All that was needed was a link – and it came in two parts. In 1787, the Arun Navigation was completed northwards from Pallingham Quay to Newbridge Wharf, near Billingshurst. Then, in 1813, Parliament authorised the Wey and Arun Junction Canal between Newbridge and Guildford. It opened in 1816 completing the link between London and the South Coast.

The price of coal in Guildford fell at once by more than 20 per cent, and the canal also carried chalk, timber and agricultural cargoes, reaching a peak of 23,000 tons in 1839. But the railways were already coming and the following year, the London and Southampton forged a new link to the South Coast. There was little immediate impact but in 1865 the London Brighton & South Coast Railway opened between Guildford and Horsham, in direct competition with the canal. Within a few years the waterway was out of business and it was formally abandoned in 1871, though the Arun Navigation struggled on until 1896.

The canal lay derelict for almost a century until, in 1970, enthusiasts established the Wey and Arun Canal Trust. Their aim was to restore navigation between London and the South Coast by reopening the waterway from Guildford to Pallingham Quay. As you'll see on your walk, they still have a mountain to climb. Long stretches remain derelict, and many bridges have been demolished. But 20 bridges and seven locks have already been rebuilt, and over a quarter of the canal's original length will soon be fully restored.

Walk 10 Directions

① From the car park, walk back towards the road for 35yds (32m) until you see a track on your left, marked by a concrete post with a small **Wey South Path** waymark near the top. Turn left, then keep right at the fork 300yds (274m) further on. Cross the tarmac drive at a public bridleway signpost and follow the waymarked path around the edge of **Fir Tree Copse**.

② The **Wey South Path** meets the canal at a gate. Turn left, and follow the tow path for 1 mile (1.6km). Notice the gentle slope as you pass the **Arun 13/Wey 10 milestone**, deep in **Sidney Wood**; it's the only clue that this overgrown section was once the site of a six lock flight.

WHAT TO LOOK FOR ℹ

The act establishing the Wey and Arun Junction Canal insisted that **milestones** must be installed every half mile along the route so that tolls could be levied accurately. All the original milestones have disappeared, but the Canal Trust is installing new ones at the original locations with a sponsorship scheme raising funds for the restoration project. You'll pass four milestones between Firfield Rough and the Sussex border.

---

③ A gravelled track crosses the canal at **Sydney Court**. Leave the tow path here and turn left, following the waymarked route across a bridleway crossroads to **High Bridge**.

④ Zig-zag right and left across **Rosemary Lane**, and rejoin the old tow path. After ½ mile (800m) look out for the **Arun 11½/Wey 11½ milestone**, and continue for 150yds (137m) until the **Sussex Border Path** crosses the canal.

⑤ Turn left, and follow the **Sussex Border Path** for 350yds (320m) until the track bends sharply right. Turn left through the metal field gate, and follow the hedge on your right. A second gate leads you past a little cottage; now, follow the public bridleway signpost that points your way through two fields, and through another gate onto a path leading out to **Rosemary Lane**. If you fancy a break, you can turn right here, for the ½ mile (800m) diversion to the **Crown** at **Alfold**.

WHERE TO EAT AND DRINK ℹ

Head for the **Crown** at Alfold for a friendly, no frills local, although they don't serve food on Sunday or Monday evenings. The canal-side **Onslow Arms** at Loxwood is open all day at weekends, serving traditional pub food and pizzas.

---

⑥ Otherwise, cross the lane and follow the waymarked bridleway for ½ mile (800m). Now turn left at the public footpath signpost; then, just a few paces past the prominent 'Riding by permit only' sign, turn right up the waymarked footpath through the woods. Fork right a short way further on, then continue over two stiles and follow the path just inside the woodland edge until it bears left and meets the **Wey South Path** at a waymark post. Turn left, and follow the path to the **Sidney Wood** car park road, before turning left again for the short distance back to your car.

WHILE YOU'RE THERE ℹ

Behind the Onslow Arms at Loxwood you'll find a restored section of the canal where you can travel on board the *Zachariah Keppel*, a 50ft (15m) narrow boat named after the contractor who built the canal. The **Wey and Arun Canal Trust** operates hourly trips on Sunday afternoons between April and October.

Walk 11

Iron Men of Brenchley

This walk from Brenchley takes you back to Kent's industrial past.

•DISTANCE•	4½ miles (7.2km)
•MINIMUM TIME•	2hrs 30min
•ASCENT / GRADIENT•	312ft (95m) ▲▲▲
•LEVEL OF DIFFICULTY•	샀 샀 샀
•PATHS•	Orchard tracks, field margins and footpaths, 14 stiles
•LANDSCAPE•	Varied, rolling landscape of orchards and hop fields
•SUGGESTED MAP•	aqua3 OS Explorer 136 The Weald, Royal Tunbridge Wells
•START / FINISH•	Grid reference: TQ 679418
•DOG FRIENDLINESS•	Good, can run free in many places
•PARKING•	Car park in Brenchley
•PUBLIC TOILETS•	At car park

BACKGROUND TO THE WALK

If you thought there was little more to Kentish history than battles with invaders and the intricacies of apple growing, this walk will soon change your mind. It starts in Brenchley, an atmospheric village with several old timbered houses, a church, pub and – a working forge. The forge, a rare sight these days, is a reminder that Kent once had a thriving iron industry and Brenchley was once at its heart.

The Iron Industry

Even before the Romans came to Britain, iron had been produced in the Weald (the wooded area) of Kent. Ore was extracted from the clay soil and roasted with charcoal (made from the trees) in a small furnace. The resulting molten iron was then hammered into shape. In the 15th and 16th centuries technology improved and large-scale, water-powered blast furnaces and hammer forges were introduced, revolutionising the industry.

Large ponds were created to provide the necessary water power and were given workmanlike names such as Hammer Pond, Pit Pond and, as in the case of the one you pass on this walk, Furnace Pond. The industry grew rapidly and brought prosperity and employment to the Weald – the ironworks at Brenchley once employed 200 men. The industry flourished until the 18th century when it moved to the coal producing regions of the north. Today Furnace Pond is a tranquil place and it's hard to believe that there was once a noisy and bustling ironworks here.

A Revolt for Social Change

A blacksmith called Wat Tyler once lived at Brenchley and gained notoriety by leading the Peasants' Revolt in 1381. This rebellion, which originated from the introduction of a hated poll tax, began in Kent and Essex and soon spread throughout the country. Tyler and his men marched to London, took control of the Tower and murdered various unpopular figures including the Archbishop of Canterbury.

The authorities were unable to take control of the mob and some semblance of calm was only restored when Richard II, then just 14, rode out to meet the rebels. He agreed to meet many of their demands and promised freedom from serfdom (peasants in those days

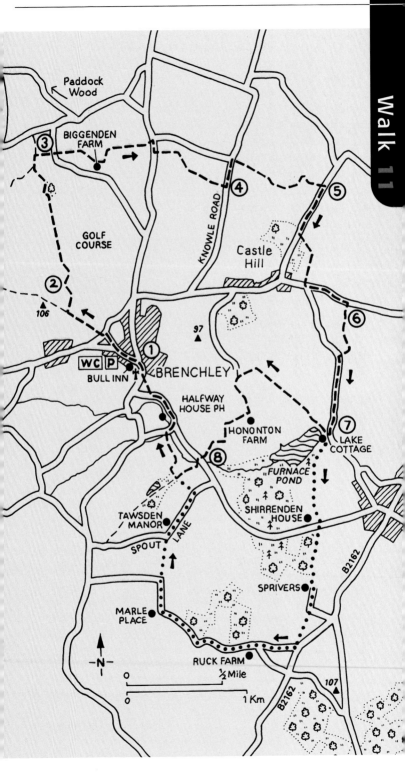

were not free but had to work for the lord of the manor). However, Tyler made further demands and was consequently killed at Smithfield, probably by the Lord Mayor of London. The authorities rapidly regained control and crushed the rebellion. The King went back on his word, serfdom was not abolished and little was gained from so much bloodshed.

Walk 11 Directions

① From the car park turn left to the war memorial. Turn right, then left at the top of the road and go up some steps into an orchard. Walk ahead, crossing two stiles, then turn left to pass some cottages. Continue through the orchard, nip over a stile and on to the **golf course**.

② Pass between the greens on the track, skirting the corner of a wood. Take the track on the right, climb a stile and join the road.

③ Walk a few paces to the right and then climb a stile on your left. Cross the field and follow the track to **Biggenden Farm**, where you cross a stile, turn left and eventually reach the road. Walk to the right and then take the path on the left. Cross a stile and the field beyond, then bear right. Continue towards the tree line and go up steps to **Knowle Road**.

④ Turn left, then, where the road bends, take the path on the right. Head across the field towards the hedge line, maintaining direction to

cross a bridge and a stile. Bear left then right over another bridge and stile, to join the road.

⑤ Turn right past some hop fields, then take a path on the left. Soon turn right through an orchard to a road. Turn left past a pond, then right on a path at a vineyard.

> ### WHERE TO EAT AND DRINK ⓘ
> The **Bull Inn** at Brenchley serves teas, coffees and sandwiches, as well as main meals. The menu features traditional English dishes and Mexican food.

⑥ Continue to a white timbered house, nip over a stile and walk between the gardens to another stile. Turn right to join the main road, then left and up to a parking area at **Furnace Pond**.

⑦ Turn right at **Lake Cottage**, right again across the bridge and walk around the pond. Join the path on the right and walk up the side of an orchard, to turn right at a waymarker. Continue across to a lane. Turn left and walk to **Hononton Farm**. Turn right along the track, through an orchard, then left at a gap in the windbreak. Turn right at the waymarker to the road.

> ### WHAT TO LOOK FOR ⓘ
> An avenue of **yew trees**, more than 400 years old, dominates the entrance to All Saints Church at Brenchley. Yew trees are a common sight in churchyards and there are many myths and legends attached to them. Some are older than the churches and indicate that the site was once used for pagan worship as yews were considered to be sacred trees.

⑧ Cross over, then take the track to your left. Follow this past the house, over a stile and turn right. Cross two more stiles and a bridge. Eventually turn right to join the road at the **Halfway House** pub. Half-way up the hill take the track on your right, cross the field and return to **Brenchley**.

Three Mills and the Canals

Discover the history of the East End waterways on this tow path walk.

•DISTANCE•	4¼ miles (6.8km)
•MINIMUM TIME•	2hrs 30min
•ASCENT / GRADIENT•	Negligible
•LEVEL OF DIFFICULTY•	
•PATHS•	Gravel, tarmac and tow paths
•LANDSCAPE•	Mainly canalside industry and housing
•SUGGESTED MAP•	aqua3 OS Explorers 162 Greenwich & Gravesend; 173 London North
•START / FINISH•	TQ 383828; near Bromley-by-Bow tube (on Explorer 173)
•DOG FRIENDLINESS•	No particular problems
•PARKING•	Tesco car park, Three Mill Lane; Bromley-by-Bow tube ¼ mile (400m)
•PUBLIC TOILETS•	At car park

BACKGROUND TO THE WALK

In the mid 19th century the banks of the River Lea were lined with flourishing industries. At that time, because it was deemed to be outside the City of London with its stringent pollution regulations, the water and surrounding air quality were dangerously poor. Since the demise of canal transport, this area, which is just a few steps away from hectic everyday life, has been transformed into a clean, peaceful haven for both walkers and wildlife.

Life Along the Lea

In the 14th century Edward III instigated a policy to encourage commercial expansion, which led to the manufacture of gunpowder, paper, soap, flour and porcelain along the Lea. These were vibrant times, but it wasn't until the 1700s that work was carried out on the meandering river to construct straight channels and build locks so that freight could be transported more easily. Some parts of east London were more significant than others in the development of the chemical industry. West Ham, for example, was just outside the jurisdiction of the Metropolitan Buildings Act of 1844 that protected the City from anti-social trades such as oil-burning and varnish making. Industry developed in Bromley-by-Bow because there was lots of cheap land and no building restrictions.

The Demise of the Waterways

As the Industrial Revolution progressed in the 19th century, the River Lea became an enormous health hazard. The factories along its banks produced a great deal of waste – the river was, in effect, used as a dumping ground for chemical and pharmaceutical waste. Looking at the scene before you today, it's not easy to picture a skyline of mass industrialism. Warehouses, cranes and gas works were here, against a backdrop of smoggy, smelly air. But, together with the noise of the powerful machinery, this would have been a way of life for many workers. For more than half of the 20th century barges still brought raw materials to the factories from London Docks, taking away the finished goods. Today, however, you're more likely to see a heron than a vessel on this stretch of the river.

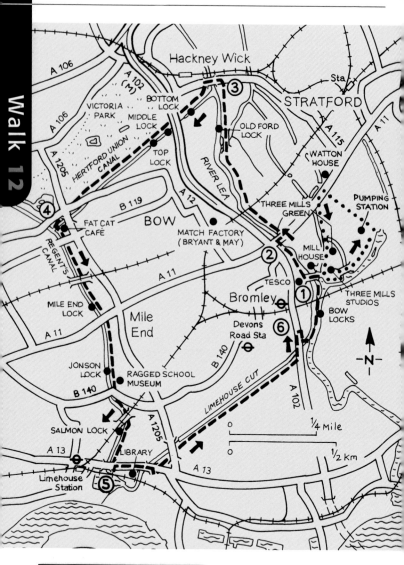

Walk 12 Directions

① From the Tesco supermarket car park in **Three Mills Lane** take the footpath to the left of an iron bridge marked 'Lee Navigation Tow Path' and 'Bow Flyover'. Continue walking ahead with the river to your right-hand side and you will shortly see the formidable volume of traffic coming into view, going across the Bow Flyover.

② Where the path ends walk up the ramp on your left, leading to the **A12**. Turn right, cross the **A11** ahead of you and turn right at the railings. Now walk down the slope and across a bridge to rejoin the tow path, with the river now to your left. Notice the brickwork of the old Bryant & May **match factory** ahead to your left. The path swings right, away from the traffic. Ignore the Greenway sign on the right and pass under two pipes that are part of the old Victorian sewer. Cross a bridge and continue along the **River Lea**, past the **Old Ford Lock**.

③ Just before the next bridge ahead, the **Hertford Union Canal** emerges and joins at a right angle on the left. Cross the bridge and turn left down a slope to join this canal along a gravel path. Pass **Bottom Lock**, **Middle Lock** and, further on, **Top Lock**. Once past the cottages of Top Lock, **Victoria Park** is visible on the right. Continue along this long, straight, paved path until you pass under **Three Colts Bridge**, a metal gate, two further bridges and another metal gate.

> **WHERE TO EAT AND DRINK** ℹ
> At the footbridge joining the Regent's Canal is Bow Wharf where you'll find the **Fat Cat Café and Bar**. A converted builders' yard, it has outside, daytime seating and a wooden interior with Chesterfield sofas. A good selection of wines, and beers include IPA and Spitfire.

④ Cross a footbridge at this T-junction of the waterways to pick up the southern section of the **Regent's Canal**, which was opened in 1820 and used by horse-drawn barges to haul coal through London. Continue along the canal, towards the blinking light of Canary Wharf. Pass under a railway bridge, **Mile End Lock**, two more bridges and **Jonson Lock**. Pass a red brick chimney, which is a sewer ventilation shaft, and walk under a

> **WHILE YOU'RE THERE** ℹ
> The **Ragged School Museum** in Copperfield Road was one of 148 schools set up by Dr Barnardo to educate poor children in London. The museum highlights the history of the East End, with a Victorian schoolroom taster session for children.

railway bridge. Continue past **Salmon Lock** and notice the viaduct ahead. After walking under **Commercial Road Bridge**, turn left and follow the steps to the road.

⑤ Turn right along **Commercial Road** and pass **Limehouse Library** and a small park on the right. Ignore the first gate on the right and instead pass over a bridge and take the steps on the right-hand side that lead down to the canal. Turn right and follow the tow path of the canal, the **Limehouse Cut**, with the water on your left. A few paces further on pass under the **A13**. Follow the tarmac path under three more bridges until it leads on to the **A102**. Walk along the pavement for 50yds (46m) and cross the road using the underpass ahead of you.

⑥ Turn right, walking with the flow of traffic, and take the first road on the left to pick up the canal path at **Bow Locks**. Walk over the concrete footbridge and under two bridges. Continue ahead towards the **Mill House**. Turn left over the bridge back to the start.

> **WHAT TO LOOK FOR** ℹ
> A Swedish manufacturer of matchsticks sold the British patent to Mr Bryant and Mr May who, in 1855, leased the **factory**, Bryant & May. A medical condition called 'phossy jaw' was common among workers and was often fatal. The fumes from the yellow phosphorous in the head of the match caused the jawbone to rot away – the smell from the diseased bone was apparently horrendous. In 1911 a new factory was built on the site; the remains have been converted into luxury flats.

Old and New in Docklands

Wandering through the Docklands, home to the world's oldest police force.

•DISTANCE•	3½ miles (5.7km)
•MINIMUM TIME•	1hr 45min
•ASCENT / GRADIENT•	Negligible
•LEVEL OF DIFFICULTY•	
•PATHS•	Paved streets and riverside paths
•LANDSCAPE•	Wharfs and docklands
•SUGGESTED MAP•	aqua3 OS Explorer 173 London North
•START•	Grid reference TQ 335807; Tower Hill tube
•FINISH•	Grid reference TQ 364803; Canary Wharf DLR
•DOG FRIENDLINESS•	On lead
•PUBLIC TOILETS•	None on route

BACKGROUND TO THE WALK

The Docklands has evolved from being one of the busiest ports in the world to being one of the most expensive dock developments. Yet there is a stillness to the area, as if the Victorian warehouses have not quite come to terms with their modern neighbours, of which the striking Canary Wharf complex is surely the best example.

While the police station in Wapping High Street is not open to the public, it is identified by the sign 'Metropolitan Police Marine Support', as the men and women here are responsible for policing the Thames. At the back of this listed building a pontoon, with its 'dead body tray' – where bodies are initially placed – sways gently on the river. Each year teams of river police and divers recover between 40 and 50 bodies and rescue more than 100 people from the river. Similar things happen on the water as on land: people get lost, things get stolen, and there are accidents and injuries. The only difference is that boats replace cars – and this watery highway is a tidal one.

In the 18th century many thousands of men worked in the docks handling imports that included fine cloth, precious metals and spices. Petty thefts were commonplace and there were around 100 pirates operating between London Bridge and Gravesend alone. Two men – John Harriott, a Justice of the Peace from Essex, and Patrick Colquhoun, a magistrate – decided to do something about it. In 1798 they obtained approval from Parliament to finance the first preventative policing of the river (the Metropolitan Police wasn't formed for another 30 years). It was a resounding success: within six months the Marine Police had saved an astounding £112,000 worth of cargo. But it wasn't until 1878, when the *Princess Alice* paddle steamer sank near Barking with the loss of over 600 lives, that the rowing galleys the Marine Police had been using were replaced with more powerful craft. Today the teams use Rigid Inflatable Boats (RIBs) and larger, more conventional vessels.

The compact museum in the police station contains some of the earliest exhibits of policing to be found. Although you must book all tours (minimum of six people), an officer will explain the interesting exhibits and show you the pontoon, and may even give their opinion of Captain Kidd. He was a fine sailor, who was hanged at nearby Execution Dock for piracy. Five years before, he had set sail for Boston but was later accused of robbing British ships and brought back to England for trial.

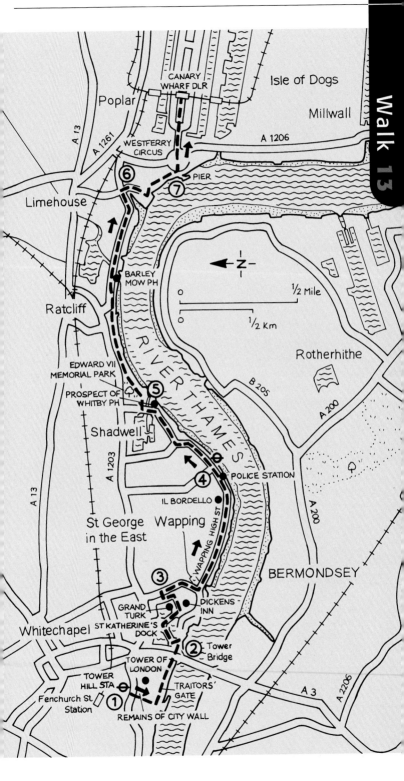

Walk 13

Walk 13 Directions

① Take the underpass from **Tower Hill tube** that leads to the **Tower of London**. In front of the moat are the remains of the east gate of the medieval wall that once surrounded the City. Turn right and follow the path, taking the exit to the right of a ticket office. Turn left through the main gates to the Tower of London and follow the cobbled path for 440yds (402m).

WHAT TO LOOK FOR ℹ

Rising to 800ft (244m), the **Canary Wharf Tower** is the flagship of the Canary Wharf development, so named because, when it was used as a dock, many of the imports were from the Canary Islands. The Tower has 50 floors and nearly 4,000 windows.

---

② Cross the road and enter **St Katherine's Dock**. Turn left, signposted 'Ivory House'. Bear right to cross a footbridge and pass some very stylish yachts and shops to cross the **Telford Footbridge**. Take the path between the *Grand Turk*, an 18th-century warship replica, and the **Dickens Inn** pub, then bear left through a private estate and right into **Mews Street**.

③ Turn right into **Thomas More Street** and, as the road swings to the right, it meets **Wapping High Street**. Turn left along this street of wharfs, luxury developments and Victorian warehouses. The blue-

---

WHILE YOU'RE THERE ℹ

Each Sunday the **White Tower** in the Tower of London holds a service at 11AM so if you time it right and arrive 15 minutes in advance, you can take part. Go to the guard house in front of the Middle Tower to gain access.

---

and-white 1970s-style building on your right is the Metropolitan Police boat yard. Continue, to pass **Il Bordello** restaurant and the **police station**.

④ Continue ahead past Wapping tube and **Wapping Lane**. After the road bends to the left at **New Crane Wharf**, turn right into **Wapping Wall**, signposted 'Thames Path'. Just past the **Prospect of Whitby** pub cross a bridge over **Shadwell Basin**.

⑤ Turn right on to the riverside path and bear to the right of the **Edward VII Memorial Park** for a superb view of Canary Wharf. After a blue apartment block the path bends away from the river and joins **Narrow Street**; it later passes the **Barley Mow** pub as you cross the **Limehouse Basin**.

⑥ Turn right into **Three Colts Street** and walk to the end, where you meet the river again at the Canary Riverside path. Continue ahead to **Canary Wharf Pier**.

WHERE TO EAT AND DRINK ℹ

You'll smell the garlic from **Il Bordello**, an Italian restaurant in Wapping High Street, long before you see it. The traditional food here is excellent. If you prefer pubs, you're really spoilt for choice. The **Dickens Inn**, St Katherine's Dock, has stripped bare boards and the **Prospect of Whitby** is one of the oldest riverside pubs in London.

---

⑦ Walk up the steps on the left of the pier, cross the road to **Westferry Circus** and continue in the direction of **Canary Wharf**, which is immediately ahead. Bear right to follow signs to Canary Wharf DLR, cutting through **Cabot Square** into **Cabot Place**, before arriving at the station entrance.

Along the River Valley to Earls Colne

A fairly challenging walk along a disused railway track, now a nature reserve, and through ancient woodland.

•DISTANCE•	6½ miles (10.4km)
•MINIMUM TIME•	3hrs 30min
•ASCENT / GRADIENT•	78ft (24m) ▲ ▲ ▲
•LEVEL OF DIFFICULTY•	🚶 🚶 🚶
•PATHS•	Grassy with some muddy tracks, forest and field-edge paths, 3 stiles
•LANDSCAPE•	Disused railway line, ancient woodland, riverside and grazing meadows
•SUGGESTED MAP•	aqua3 OS Explorer 195 Braintree & Saffron Walden
•START / FINISH•	Grid reference: TL 855290
•DOG FRIENDLINESS•	Some stiles only suitable for chihuahuas, bigger dogs will need to be lifted
•PARKING•	Free parking at Queens Road car park in Earls Colne
•PUBLIC TOILETS•	Queens Road car park

BACKGROUND TO THE WALK

Is this the loveliest valley in all Essex? Judge for yourself as you follow the meandering River Colne and visit the delightful village of Earls Colne where the de Vere family, Earls of Oxford and one of the greatest families in English history, left their name. Here you will find a lovely view from the split-timber seating beside St Andrew's Church, with its tower visible for miles around; a nature reserve along a disused railway track, which has been cut back allowing wildlife to flourish, and the ancient woodlands of Chalkney Woods.

A Disused Railway Line

The Colne Valley Railway opened in 1860 and soon brought prosperity to the valley. Earls Colne, one of the stations on the line, was built by the Hunt family who developed the Atlas Works, which produced farming equipment until it closed in 1988. The line was used to import raw materials and to despatch the finished product, but since its closure in 1965 the track side vegetation has become a rich habitat for wildlife, with plenty of trees and shrubs providing heavy shade. As you walk along the disused track you will see evidence of coppicing which allows light to reach the ground, which in turn allows wildlife such as butterflies and other insects to proliferate.

Chalkney Wood dates back to 1605 when it was owned by the de Vere family. This walk takes you through the woods where conifers are gradually being replaced with traditional species to regenerate the woodland. You'll also see, near the kennels, an 18th-century watermill which last worked in the 1930s and is now a private residence. In the Alder Valley are the remains of conifer plantations established in the 1960s, but today the area supports more moss and liverworts than any other wood in East Anglia. You'll also pass close to the Wool Track, believed to be an ancient Roman road linking Colchester and Cambridge, and come across a prominent bank which enclosed the woods as a swine park where pigs would feed on acorns amongst the coppice.

Brickfields and Long Meadow Nature Reserve, bordered by woodland of oak, ash and hawthorn, has plenty of boggy areas and wet grassland. It is small, but has plenty of insect life. The ponds, surrounded by acacia and rhododendron, are home to newts, frogs and dragonflies. A major feature of the area is the anthills, which house huge colonies of yellow ants. Long Meadow, used for grazing, is free of fertilisers and pesticides, and as a result supports plenty of wildlife and a variety of grasses such as yarrow and birds trefoil. Near by you should also find a rare surviving elm tree.

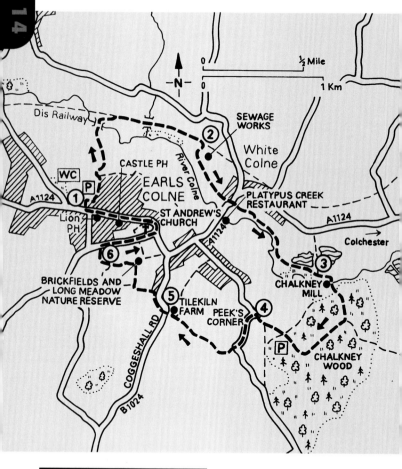

Walk 14 **Directions**

① From the car park, turn left and left again into **Burrows Road**. Cross **Hilly Bunnies Road** and maintain direction to the **Wildside waymark**. Here bear slightly right, then left on to the cross-field path, downhill

across the golf course. Cross the footbridge following the yellow waymark over the **River Colne**. Follow the path for 70yds (64m) and bear left on the lesser path towards trees to the waymarked stile and information board marking the entrance to the railway nature reserve. Turn right on to the railway embankment and maintain direction keeping the river and golf course on your right. Cross the footbridge over the **River Peb** and maintain your direction for about 600yds (549m).

② Leave the reserve by turning right at a collection of waymarks. Keep the fence of the sewage works on your left and follow the grassy path to reach **Colne Ford Road**. Turn left, cross the road, and follow the footpath and waymark between house Nos 20 and 22 through the wooden gate. Maintain direction across the meadow with the **River Colne** down on your right until you climb stile No 2.

> **WHERE TO EAT AND DRINK** ℹ️
> A good selection of eateries can be found in the High Street. Choose from the **Colne Valley Tandoori** restaurant which serves an 'eat-as-much-as-you-like' buffet on Sunday evenings or relax with your tired dog in the garden of the **Castle** pub. In Colneford Road you can enjoy a meal and drink at the **Platypus Creek** restaurant by the River Colne.

③ Turn right and cross the bridge over the Colne, passing kennels and **Chalkney Mill** on your right, and maintain direction into **Chalkney Wood**. Walk for 300yds (274m), take the second path on your right and go along the straight bridleway, bounded on the left by Corsican pine. Maintain direction for 500yds (457m) and bear right to the parking area. Take the wide downhill track for 300yds (274m) and turn left into **Tey Road** at **Peek's Corner**.

④ After 300yds (274m) turn right at the fingerpost and go along the field-edge path keeping the hedgerows on your right. Cross the

> **WHAT TO LOOK FOR** ℹ️
> The de Veres were great crusaders and were associated with a legendary silver star which was won outside the walls of Antioch on their first crusade. The family left their mark in the form of a star on buildings in this area of Essex, leaving no one in any doubt as to who owned and constructed them. One of these buildings is the unique star-studded tower of **St Andrew's Church**.

earth bridge through trees, maintain direction uphill, and pass Tilekiln Farm, on your right, to **Coggeshall Road**.

⑤ Turn right at Coggeshall Road and after 200yds (183m) turn left at the fingerpost marked **Park Lane**. Follow the path through the kissing gate and turn immediately right along the path bounded by thick gorse bushes. Follow the path left and downhill, keeping woods on your right, until you reach the **Wildside** waymarked stile. Cross the stile and walk along the field-edge path, keeping the hedgerow on your right, to an earth bridge where you turn right over the stream.

⑥ Take the path past a Brickfields information board on your right and turn right into **Park Lane** with St Andrews Church on your left. Turn left into **Coggeshall Road** and the **High Street** and return to the car park.

> **WHILE YOU'RE THERE** ℹ️
> If you're driving, head up to the **East Anglian Railway Museum** at Chappel Station to view a fine collection of goods and passenger rolling stock. Railway enthusiasts and children alike will love the interactive signal boxes and video displays in this working museum which covers a century of railway engineering in East Anglia.

Walk 15

Halstead's Courtaulds Connection

A charming town and country walk discovering the influence of the Courtauld family and their textile legacy.

•DISTANCE•	3 miles (4.8km)
•MINIMUM TIME•	1hr 15min
•ASCENT / GRADIENT•	90ft (27m) ▲▲ ▲
•LEVEL OF DIFFICULTY•	鼎 鼎 鼎
•PATHS•	Town streets and grassy tracks
•LANDSCAPE•	Urban, river and meadow
•SUGGESTED MAP•	aqua3 OS Explorer 195 Braintree & Saffron Walden
•START / FINISH•	Grid reference: TL 812306
•DOG FRIENDLINESS•	Pleasant on-lead town walk but most dogs will prefer the meadow
•PARKING•	Pay-and-display in Chapel Street and Mill Bridge
•PUBLIC TOILETS•	Chapel Street

BACKGROUND TO THE WALK

Surrounded by the gentle rolling countryside of the Colne Valley in north Essex, Halstead developed over many centuries as a busy market town and, in the Middle Ages, much of its prosperity came from the wool trade. In the early 19th century Samuel Courtauld (1793–1881), an industrious and successful businessman, brought a new lease of life to the town. A descendant of a Huguenot refugee family, he set up in business as a silk throwster (a person who twists silk fibres into thread) and his family went on to found the internationally known Courtaulds company.

A Royal Trendsetter

Courtaulds had its share of ups and downs, but always seemed one step ahead of its competitors, due to a policy of diversification. When the silk industry dwindled, mainly due to French competition, the company specialised in the production of mourning crêpe, which was to become the definitive fashion material during, and after, Queen Victoria's reign (1837–1901). When crêpe fell out of favour, Courtaulds turned to the manufacture of artificial silk which became such a success that brand name materials such as Celanese saw the company through the depression of the 1930s.

The Courtaulds connection with Halstead began in 1825 when Samuel Courtauld bought the present Townsford Mill and converted it to produce silk-woven fabrics; much of the raw material was imported in bulk from India. In those days the cloth was produced in the workers' homes and some of these early weavers' cottages can still be seen next to the mill in Bridge Street. By 1891 the mill became one of England's largest employers, where 1,400 people, the vast majority young girls and women, toiled at 1,000 looms.

The Courtauld family left legacies throughout Halstead and on this walk you will discover some of them, such as the Jubilee Fountain at the top of Market Street, on a spot previously occupied by the old Market Cross. In Hedingham Lane you can see the

Courtaulds workers' houses which are named after characters and titles from Jane Austen's novels. The family also footed the bill for building Halstead Cottage Hospital while the Homes of Rest next door, a semi-circular row of single-storey dwellings built in 1923, provided much-needed housing for retired silk weavers.

Courtauld Institute

Samuel Courtauld became very rich, and lived to the ripe old age of 88 in an impressive Tudor mansion called Gosfield Hall, a few miles from Halstead. During the 1920s his great-nephew and namesake would often drive or walk along Box Mill where he apparently took a dislike to the housing and duly replaced them with his own preferred style of cottages. The young Samuel (1876–1947) went on to establish the Courtauld Institute of Art in London before he died. In 1982 Courtaulds factory finally closed down but there's little doubt that this name lives on in Halstead.

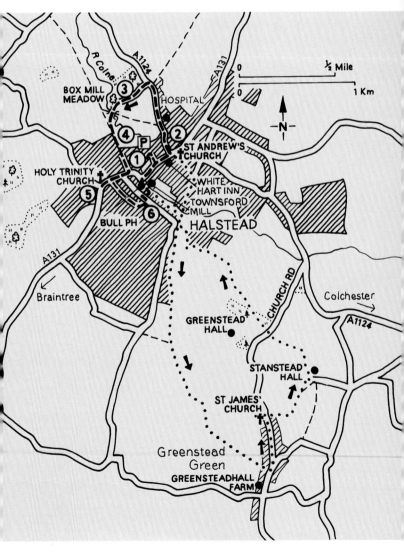

Walk 15 Directions

① Turn right into **Chapel Street** then left into the **High Street** by the post office. Walk up **Market Hill** to the **Jubilee Fountain** for panoramic views of the layout of the town and note the distant Mount Hill, proof that not all of Essex is flat.

② Turn left into **Hedingham Road** (A1124) passing Halstead Hospital and the Courtauld Homes of Rest on your right. Turn left into **Box Mill Lane** where several cottages and larger dwellings attest to further building by the Courtaulds.

WHAT TO LOOK FOR ⓘ

Three-storeyed weavers' homes were still fairly common in Halstead during the 19th and early 20th centuries. Some of these survive in **Weavers Row** near Parsonage Street. The upper and lower floors were used as domestic quarters while the middle floor, which had one room extending the length of the row, was used as a weaving workshop.

---

③ At the end of Box Mill Lane, maintain direction into **Box Mill Meadow**, a fine picnic spot, and cross the footbridge over the **River Colne** as it flows south into the town. Along the river bank, traces of rubble are all that remain of the two mills, one a watermill and the other wind powered, that once occupied this spot. Take the footpath to the left.

WHILE YOU'RE THERE ⓘ

Some of the oldest houses in Halstead, dating back to the 14th century, can be seen at the bottom of Chapel Hill. At the top of the High Street is the flint and rubble St Andrew's Church with its lovely tower; some parts date back to the 15th century.

---

④ At the edge of **Halstead Town Football Ground**, cross the stile and maintain your direction along the footpath which becomes a grassy track, the former route of the Halstead and Colne Valley Railway. Go straight ahead into **Butler Road**, which was named after R A Butler (1902–82), better known as Rab, Conservative politician and Member of Parliament for Saffron Walden. At the T-junction with **Trinity Street** notice the redevelopment across the road, where flats and a park area called Trinity Court now stand on the site of the old railway station.

⑤ Turn right and walk to **Trinity Church** on your right. Close by are some of the oldest houses in the town. Retrace your steps for a few paces and turn right just after the police station into **New Street**. Note the public gardens opposite the Methodist church, turn left into **Martin Street**, then left again and right into **Factory Lane West** by the tourist information office.

⑥ Turn left into **The Causeway**, Courtaulds old Townsford Mill on the right, and walk ahead into **Bridge Street.** Turn right to cross the bridge over the River Colne and go into the **High Street** to the post office. Pause here awhile to note the varied architecture around you. Walk along **Chapel Street** and return to the car park.

WHERE TO EAT AND DRINK ⓘ

You are spoilt for choice with a range of tea rooms, restaurants and pubs. Of particular historic interest are two 500-year-old coaching inns in the High Street: the **White Hart** which ran a regular service to Great Yarmouth and the **Bull Hotel,** which featured in the TV series *Lovejoy* starring Ian McShane.

Witney – from Town to Country

Discover Witney's many treasures before heading for a popular country park on the town's outskirts.

•DISTANCE•	3½ miles (5.7km)
•MINIMUM TIME•	1hr 30min
•ASCENT / GRADIENT•	Negligible
•LEVEL OF DIFFICULTY•	𝕩𝕩 𝕩𝕩 𝕩𝕩
•PATHS•	Pavements, meadow and waterside paths, 1 stile
•LANDSCAPE•	Urban, country park and waterside on town outskirts
•SUGGESTED MAP•	aqua3 OS Explorer 180 Oxford
•START / FINISH•	Grid reference: SP 357096
•DOG FRIENDLINESS•	Busy streets at start and finish. Under control or on lead in Witney Lake and Meadows Country Park
•PARKING•	Public car park by Woolgate Shopping Centre, off Witan Way
•PUBLIC TOILETS•	Woolgate Shopping Centre, recreation ground and Cogges Manor Farm Museum (for visitors)

BACKGROUND TO THE WALK

Unlike Burford and Broadway, Witney never established itself as a Cotswold honeypot. Perhaps it is just as well. It is a place to stumble on, to be discovered without the fuss of coach parties and souvenir hunters. Stroll through its picturesque streets and you'll find a great deal of charm and character. It is attractive without being twee, smart without being 'touristy'. In short, it is classic Middle England. One of Witney's best views is from Church Green, looking across to the parish church at the southern end. This quiet corner of the town has the feel of a small English cathedral city and if Witney were ever descended upon by tourism marketing men, the focus of their attention would surely be here.

Witney's Famous Blankets

Perhaps the main reason the town never became a major attraction is its industrial past. During the Middle Ages Witney became the centre of a thriving woollen trade. It was the famous Cotswold sheep and the meandering River Windrush that contributed to the town's success – the river proved to be eminently suitable for the scouring of the woollen cloth. Fortunately, the townsfolk knew how to yield the best from these attributes and in later years Witney became famous throughout the world for producing blankets.

It was in 1669 that Richard Early apprenticed his teenage son, Thomas, to the woollen trade. The boy lived up to his father's expectations and by 1688 he was one of the town's leading master weavers. He was so successful that he was chosen to present a pair of gold-fringed blankets to James II. In 1711 the Witney weavers were granted a charter to form a Company of Blanket Weavers. This signifcant development, though long overdue, was welcomed by the district's weaving community, and weavers operating within a 20-mile (32km) radius of the town were required to bring their blankets to the company's headquarters to be inspected and hallmarked.

Thomas Early became the first master of the company and in later years the Early family presented blankets to King George III and Queen Charlotte as part of their royal visit to Oxfordshire in 1788. However, it wasn't long before the Industrial Revolution got under way and the wind of change began to blow through Witney, as innovative machinery ushered in a new era in the manufacturing industries. The traditional weavers feared for their jobs and riots broke out in the streets. But it was to no avail – in spite of all the protests, the new order was here to stay.

In 1960 Witney's two major blanket manufacturers merged, consolidating an association already forged by intermarriage between the two families. With the eventual closure of the company, Witney's famous tradition for producing blankets now lies at the core of the town's industrial heritage.

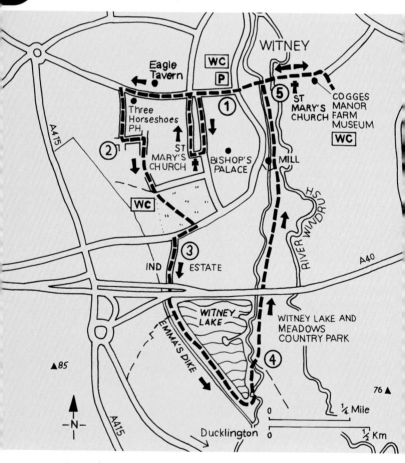

Walk 16 **Directions**

① Turn right into **Langdale Gate** and walk along towards the **Butter Cross**. Turn left immediately before

it and walk down the left side of **Church Green**. Have a look at the remains of the **Bishop's Palace** and then visit **St Mary's Church** next door. With your back to the church, walk along the left side of Church

Walk 16

Green and turn left at the Butter Cross into **Corn Street**. Keep ahead and, when the street becomes pleasantly tree-lined, cutting between handsome houses, turn left just beyond the **Three Horseshoes** pub into **The Crofts**. Follow the road between terraced stone houses, evoking the days when Witney was a thriving mill town.

> **WHERE TO EAT AND DRINK**
> The Eagle Tavern in Corn Street is one among many pubs in Witney. Expect a good and inexpensive range of meals and snacks. Alternatively, there are several cafés and restaurants in the town.

② Follow **The Crofts** to the left and turn right at the end. Keep a stone wall on the left and walk along to **St Mary's Court**. Continue ahead along an alleyway, with a school and the spire of St Mary's on the left and, when you reach the corner of a recreation ground, keep to its right edge, passing a toilet block. Turn right at the road, then turn first left at the pedestrian lights into **Station Lane**.

③ Follow the road through an industrial estate and take the path at the end, beneath the **A40**. Avoid a footbridge on the right and walk ahead through a kissing gate. The walk now cuts between **Witney Lake** and surrounding meadows,

> **WHAT TO LOOK FOR**
> **Witney Lake and Meadows Country Park** covers 75 acres (30ha) and includes the site of a large former gravel pit, two streams of the River Windrush and fields of hay and meadowland. Acquired by Witney Town Council in 1988, the country park is home to many different species of wildlife, including tawny owls, sparrowhawks, butterflies and damselflies.

part of a country park. Continue along the lakeside path, with the houses of Ducklington seen over to the right beyond an area of scrub. Keep **Emma's Dike** left and curve to the left. The lake is still clearly seen, as is Witney church spire at intervals in the distance. On the right is the **River Windrush**. Make for a large concrete bridge and cross it, branching left to a kissing gate.

④ Keep the field boundary over to your left and look for a kissing gate by the **A40**. Pass under it again to another kissing gate and head north to a stile, keeping your back to the main road. Cross over to a gate and keep ahead with office buildings seen on the left. Pass under power lines to two kissing gates and a notice board. Keep ahead, passing to the right of a dilapidated mill which originally had its own undershot wheels. Follow the path between margins of vegetation and eventually you reach a spur path to **Cogges Manor Farm Museum**.

> **WHILE YOU'RE THERE**
> Visit the **Cogges Manor Farm Museum**, which illustrates how this 20-acre (8.1ha) site would have looked in the Victorian era, with traditional breeds of animals, original farm buildings and displays of farm implements and machinery. Daily demonstrations of domestic and farm work take place in the manor house, dairy and farmyard.

⑤ To visit the museum, turn right and follow the path and adjoining cycleway to the Priory and St Mary's Church. Continue to the adjoining museum and then retrace your steps, heading now for Witney town centre. Pass an electricity sub station on the right and walk along to the road. Cross over into **Langdale Gate** and return to the car park.

Hook Norton's Towering Success

Explore delightful ironstone country before visiting one of Oxfordshire's more unusual buildings.

•DISTANCE•	4½ miles (7.2km)
•MINIMUM TIME•	2hrs
•ASCENT / GRADIENT•	164ft (50m)
•LEVEL OF DIFFICULTY•	
•PATHS•	Field paths, tracks and bridleways, quiet roads
•LANDSCAPE•	Undulating countryside close to Warwickshire border
•SUGGESTED MAP•	aqua3 OS Explorer 191 Banbury, Bicester & Chipping Norton
•START / FINISH•	Grid reference: SP 355330
•DOG FRIENDLINESS•	Under control on farmland and on lead where requested
•PARKING•	Spaces in Hook Norton village centre
•PUBLIC TOILETS•	Hook Norton Brewery Visitor Centre

BACKGROUND TO THE WALK

Hook Norton is one of those places that you are most likely to stumble upon by accident. Hidden away down winding lanes a few miles from the Cotswold town of Chipping Norton, this sizeable village, one of the largest parishes in Oxfordshire, is typical of many other settlements in the county – with one possible exception.

Tucked away in Brewery Lane, on the edge of the village, is the Hook Norton Brewery, displaying one of the most distinctive and unusual Victorian façades in the country. The tower brewing building, erected at the turn of the last century, has been described as 'an essay in brick, ironstone, slate, weather-boarding, half timber and cast iron.'

Following Tradition

During the 19th century it was traditional for most towns, cities and even large villages to have their own brewery. During the 1880s Oxfordshire alone had almost 50. Today, the scarcity of independent breweries reflects the changing fortunes of the licensed trade. However, the Hook Norton Brewery has managed to fight off the big corporate companies and remain successful.

It was during the Victorian era, in 1849, that John Harris set up in business as a maltster by brewing beer in a nearby farmhouse. A year later, Harris built his own brewhouse, where he used pure Cotswold spring water. He soon found there was a great demand for his beer and so he established a small brewery with its own maltings.

Growing the Business

When Harris died, his son and nephew assumed responsibility for the running of the business and by 1899 work on the present tower brewery was complete. The new building, comprising six floors, housed the latest brewing equipment and allowed the entire brewing sequence to be undertaken as a continuous process. It was at this time that John Harris and

Company became the Hook Norton Brewery Company Limited. Following the death of John Harris, the task of running the brewery fell to his son-in-law Alban Clarke, who was killed in a motorcycle accident in 1917. Hook Norton remains a family business in the 21st century. The brewery is now run by Clarke's grandson, David, while his son, James, is Head Brewer and a director of the company.

There is nothing brash or hi-tech about Hook Norton. Much of the brewery's intricate machinery is original – the process of brewing has been the same for over 100 years and apart from a new laboratory, stainless-steel copper and cooling system, little has changed. One of the brewery's greatest assets is the mighty steam-driven, 25-horse-power piston engine, dating back to 1899. Today the Hook Norton Brewery has 42 tied houses and 42 employees. In September 1999, 100 years after brewing began in the existing building, Princess Anne opened a new visitor centre and museum, housed in the original maltings.

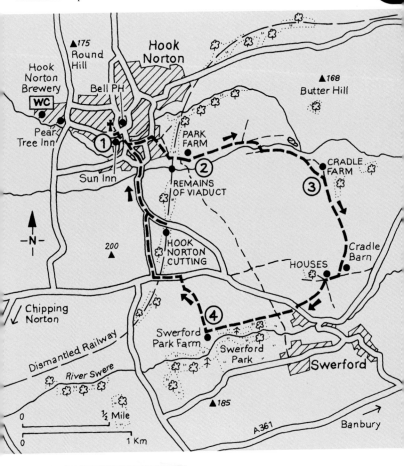

Walk 17 Directions

① With the church on your left, turn right into **Middle Hill**. Follow it down to the next road and keep

ahead to the bridge. Turn left into **Park Road** and follow it to the next junction. Continue ahead, keeping a row of bungalows on the left. When the road bends sharp left, join a waymarked bridleway and follow it

Walk 17

out of Hook Norton. Pass the remains of the old railway viaduct and walk along to **Park Farm**.

② Cross a cattle grid and continue for about 50yds (46m). When the track forks, keep left and follow the path to a gate. Continue along the field edge to the next gate and follow the obvious track as it curves to the right. Cross a ford at the footbridge and make for the next gate. Follow the field boundary and cross into the next field, keeping trees and a hedgerow on the left. Head for a galvanised gate and swing right at the bridleway sign. Head diagonally across the field and look for a gate in the trees in the top boundary. Follow the grassy path alongside the fence to reach a drive.

WHERE TO EAT AND DRINK ⓘ

There are several pubs to choose from in Hook Norton. The **Sun Inn** and the **Bell** both serve food and are both situated in the village centre. On the outskirts of Hook Norton, close to the brewery, lies the **Pear Tree Inn**, a brewery house since 1869. Low ceilings, beams and horse brasses add to the charm and character of the bar and outside is a popular beer garden. Light refreshments are served at the **Hook Norton Brewery Visitor Centre**.

---

③ Turn right here, away from **Cradle Farm**, and walk along to some outbuildings at the point where the drive bends sharp left. Keep right here and follow the track

alongside a pair of semi-detached houses on the right. Emerge from the trees to three tracks; take the middle track up the slope between fences to reach the road. Cross over to a galvanised gate and follow the bridleway between fences, trees and paddocks. On reaching a gate turn right to a wrought-iron gate leading into a field. Turn left and make for a further gate into the next field. Pass to the right-hand side of some fencing and make for a gate in the field boundary.

④ Turn right to join an avenue of lime trees. At length the drive reaches the road. Turn left, then take the first right for Hook Norton. At the first junction, turn right at the sign for Swerford and walk along to **Hook Norton Cutting**. Retrace your steps to the junction and continue ahead towards **Hook Norton**. Pass the speed restriction sign and keep ahead into the village. Pass **Park Road** on the right and take **Middle Hill** back up to the church and the pubs.

WHAT TO LOOK FOR ⓘ

As you leave Hook Norton, near the start of the walk, keep an eye out for the remains of an old **railway viaduct** on the disused Banbury-to-Cheltenham line. Seven stone pillars serve as a sad reminder of the golden age of rail travel. A key factor in the success of the brewery during its early years was the welcome presence of navvies who were engaged in the building of the line between 1865 and 1888.

WHILE YOU'RE THERE ⓘ

Tours of the **Hook Norton Brewery** are by prior arrangement and take place in the morning. Take a stroll along to the **Hook Norton Cutting**, now a nature reserve. The site is managed by the local wildlife trust, the only voluntary organisation in the region concerned with all aspects of local wildlife conservation. The wildlife trust manages more than 90 reserves within the Oxfordshire, Berkshire and Buckinghamshire region, which are the haunt of rare and endangered species.

Stanton and Stanway from Snowshill

Discovering three of Gloucestershire's finest villages, which were saved from decline and decay.

•DISTANCE•	6¼ miles (10.1km)
•MINIMUM TIME•	2hrs 45min
•ASCENT / GRADIENT•	625ft (190m) ▲▲▲
•LEVEL OF DIFFICULTY•	🚶 🚶 🚶
•PATHS•	Tracks, estate grassland and pavement
•LANDSCAPE•	High grassland, open wold, wide-ranging views and villages
•SUGGESTED MAP•	aqua3 OS Explorer OL45 The Cotswolds
•START / FINISH•	Grid reference: SP 096337
•DOG FRIENDLINESS•	On leads – livestock on most parts of walk
•PARKING•	Snowshill village
•PUBLIC TOILETS•	None on route

BACKGROUND TO THE WALK

The villages of the Cotswolds are radiant examples of English vernacular architecture, but they have not always been the prosperous places they are today. Many, like Stanton and Snowshill, were once owned by the great abbeys. With the dissolution of the monasteries they became the property of private landlords. Subsistence farmers were edged out by the introduction of short leases and enclosure of the open fields. Villagers who had farmed their own strips of land became labourers. The number of small farmers decreased dramatically and, with the innovations of the Industrial Revolution, so too did the demand for labour. Cheaper food flooded in from overseas and several catastrophic harvests compounded the problem.

To the Cities

People left the countryside in droves to work in the industrial towns and cities. Cotswold villages, once at the core of the most important woollen industry in medieval Europe, gradually became impoverished backwaters. But the villages themselves resisted decay. Unlike villages in many other parts of Britain, their buildings were made of stone. Enlightened landlords, who cherished their innate beauty, turned them into huge restoration projects.

Enlightened Landlords

The three villages encountered on this walk are living reminders of this process. Snowshill, together with Stanton, was once owned by Winchcombe Abbey. In 1539 it became the property of Henry VIII's sixth wife, Catherine Parr. The manor house was transformed into the estate's administrative centre and remained in the Parr family until 1919. Then the estate was bought by Charles Wade, a sugar plantation owner. He restored the house and devoted his time to amassing an extraordinary collection of art and artefacts, which he subsequently bequeathed to the National Trust. Now forming the basis of a museum, his collection, from Japanese armour to farm machinery, is of enormous appeal. Next on this walk comes Stanway, a small hamlet at the centre of a large estate owned by Lord Neidpath. The most striking feature here is the magnificent gatehouse to the Jacobean Stanway House, a gem of Cotswold architecture built around 1630.

Restored Houses

The village of Stanton comes last on this walk. It was rescued from decay and oblivion in 1906 by the architect Sir Philip Stott. He bought and restored Stanton Court and many of the village's 16th-century houses. The peaceful parish church is located along a lane leading from the market cross. It has two pulpits (one dating from the 14th-century, the other Jacobean) and a west gallery added by the Victorian restorer Sir Ninian Comper. The founder of Methodism, John Wesley, preached here in 1733.

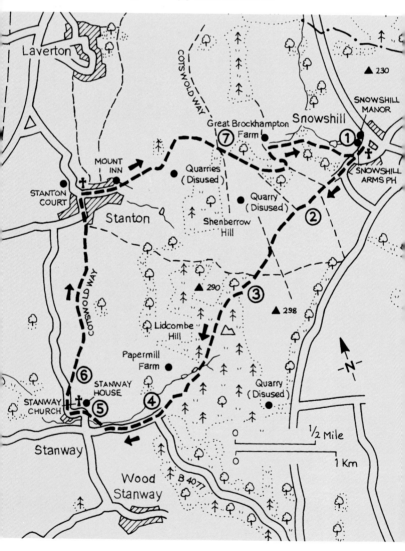

Walk 18 Directions

① Walk out of Snowshill village with the **church** on your left. After ¼ mile (400m) turn right, down a lane. After another ¼ mile (400m), at a corner, turn left up to a gate and enter a field.

② Go quarter left to a gate. In the next field go half right to the far corner and left along a track. Take the second footpath on the right through a gate into a field and walk across to another field. Cross this to a track.

WHAT TO LOOK FOR ℹ️

As you pass through Stanway, look to the left before you mount the stile. You'll see the cricket pitch and, overlooking it, a **thatched pavilion**. This was presented to Stanway at the beginning of the 20th century by J M Barrie, creator of Peter Pan, a keen cricketer and a regular visitor to Stanway House.

---

③ Walk down the track. After 275yds (251m) turn right on to a stony track, descending steeply through **Lidcombe Wood**. Where it flattens out a farm will come into view across fields to the right, after which the track bears left. Continue straight on along a narrow footpath to a road.

④ Walk along the pavement and, after 500yds (457m), turn right over a stile into a small **orchard**. Walk across this, bearing slightly right, to arrive at a gate. Go through this and walk with a high wall to your right, to reach a road.

⑤ Turn right and pass the impressive entrance to **Stanway House** and **Stanway church**. Follow the road as it goes right. Shortly after another entrance turn right over a stile. Go half left to another stile and in the next large field go half right.

⑥ Now walk all the way into **Stanton**, following the regular and clear waymarkers of the Cotswold Way. After 1 mile (1.6km) you will arrive at a stile at the edge of Stanton. Turn left along a track to a junction. Turn right here and walk through the village. Where the road goes left, walk straight on, passing the stone cross and then another footpath. Climb up to pass the **Mount Inn**. Behind it walk up a steep, shaded path to a gate. Then walk straight up the hill (ignoring a path to the right after a few paces). Climb all the way to the top to meet a lane.

⑦ Walk down the lane for 250yds (229m) then turn left over a stile into woodland. Follow the path, going left at a fork. At the bottom cross a stile on to a lane and turn left. Walk along here for 200yds (183m). Before a cottage turn right over a stile into a scrubby field. Cross to the far side and turn right through a gate. Continue to a stile on your right, cross it and turn left. Follow the margin of this grassy area to a gate and then follow the path back into **Snowshill**.

WHILE YOU'RE THERE ℹ️

Even those who usually shun museums should make an exception for the one at **Snowshill Manor**, which is more like a fantastical toyshop than a museum. Although the manor is near the heart of the village, the entrance is outside it, on the Broadway road. **Stanway House** has restricted opening hours but is similarly worth a visit – anything less like the conventional picture of a stately home is hard to imagine.

Walk 19

Sapperton, Daneway and the Thames & Severn Canal

Sapperton, both the focus of a major engineering project and a cradle for cultural change.

•DISTANCE•	6 miles (9.7km)
•MINIMUM TIME•	3hrs
•ASCENT / GRADIENT•	345ft (105m) ▲ ▲ ▲
•LEVEL OF DIFFICULTY•	🚶 🚶 🚶
•PATHS•	Woodland paths and tracks, fields, lanes and canalside paths, 12 stiles
•LANDSCAPE•	Secluded valleys and villages
•SUGGESTED MAP•	aqua3 OS Explorer 168 Stroud, Tetbury and Malmesbury
•START / FINISH•	Grid reference: SO 948033
•DOG FRIENDLINESS•	Good – very few livestock
•PARKING•	In Sapperton village near church
•PUBLIC TOILETS•	None on route

BACKGROUND TO THE WALK

Sapperton was at the centre of two conflicting tendencies during the late 18th and early 20th centuries – the Industrial Revolution and the Romantic Revival. In the first case, it was canal technology that came to Sapperton. Canal construction was widespread throughout England from the mid-18th century onwards. Just as 'dot com' companies attracted vast sums of money in the late 1990s, so investors poured their money into 18th-century joint stock companies, regardless of their profitability. Confidence was high and investors expected to reap the rewards of commercial success based on the need to ship goods swiftly across the country.

Tunnel Vision

One key project was thought to be the canal that would link the River Severn and the River Thames. The main obstacle was the need for a tunnel through the Cotswolds, the cost of which could be unpredictable. But these were heady days and investors' money was forthcoming to press ahead with the scheme in 1783. During the tunnel's construction, the diarist and traveller John Byng visited the workings. With obvious distaste he wrote, 'I was enveloped in thick smoke arising from the gunpowder of the miners, at whom, after passing by many labourers who work by small candles, I did at last arrive; they come from the Derbyshire and Cornish mines, are in eternal danger and frequently perish by falls of earth'.

The Thames and Severn Canal opened in 1789, linking the Thames at Lechlade with the Stroudwater Navigation at Stroud. The Sapperton Tunnel, at 3,400yds (3,109m) long, is still one of the longest transport tunnels in the country. Barges were propelled through the tunnel by means of 'leggers', who 'walked' against the tunnel walls and who patronised the inns that are at both tunnel entrances. Yet the canal was not a success: either there was too much or too little water; rock falls and leakages required constant attention. The cost of maintaining the tunnel led to the closure of the canal in 1911.

The Arts and Crafts Movement

It isn't just the tunnel that is of interest in Sapperton. Some of the cottages here were built by disciples of William Morris (1834–96). He was the doyen of the Arts and Crafts Movement. It aspired to reintroduce to English life a simple yet decorative functionality, a reaction to the growing mass-production methods engendered by the Industrial Revolution. Furniture makers and architects like Ernest Gimson (from Leicestershire), Sidney and Ernest Barnsley (from Birmingham), and Norman Jewson all worked in Daneway, at Daneway House. Gimson and the Barnsley brothers are buried at Sapperton church. The finest example of their vernacular-style architecture in Sapperton is Upper Dorval House. The entrance to the western end of the Sapperton Tunnel is in fact in the hamlet of Daneway, a short walk along the path from the Daneway Inn, formerly called the Bricklayer's Arms. Daneway House, the 14th-century house that was let to followers of William Morris by Earl Bathurst, is a short distance up the road from the pub.

Walk 19

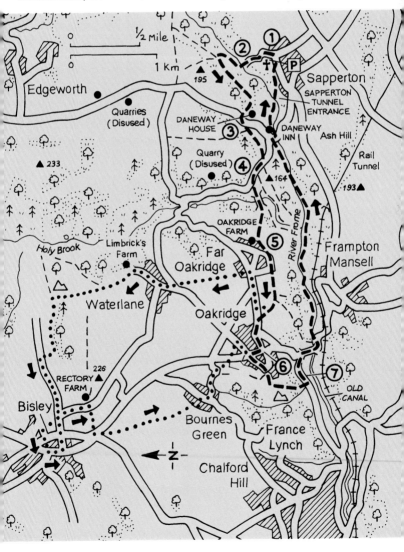

Walk 19

Walk 19 Directions

① With the church to your left, walk along a 'No Through Road'. This descends rapidly and, at the entrance to a house at the bottom, turn left on to a footpath.

② Continue uphill into **woodland**. Take the main path, ignoring a footpath on the left, but where it then forks, go left uphill. Climb to a junction of tracks. Turn left and stay on the track for ½ mile (800m) to a gate at a lane.

③ Turn left and then immediately right over a stile (opposite **Daneway House**). Take the first left and walk along a wide grassy area, with a fence to the right, to a stile at a lane. Turn right for 250yds (229m) then turn left over a stile.

④ Walk down a drive. Just before the house go left through a hedge and turn immediately right, following a path to a stile. Cross this, then a bridge and a field, and a stile into woodland. Follow a path to a gate at a field, which you cross half right. Pass through a gate and head left of **Oakridge Farm** to another gate on to a lane.

⑤ Turn left and pass a junction. At a sharp right corner go ahead into a field. Walk to a stile on the far side. Cross the next field and find a stile in the top right corner. Follow the left margin of the next field to a road. Turn left along the road through **Oakridge**.

⑥ At a crossroads turn right, climbing to a road. Turn left. At the **green** go to the end and bear right to a stile. Enter a field, keep close to a hedge on the left and cross two further stiles. Bear right across a field to a stile into woodland. Descend steeply and turn left on to a path, which you follow to a junction. Turn left down to a road.

⑦ Turn left then, at a junction, turn right to cross a bridge. Bear left and, a few paces after, turn left again over a footbridge then right on to a footpath. Follow the canal for 600yds (549m). Cross a bridge and turn left on a path to a road by the **Daneway Inn**. Turn right and then left to continue by the canal to the **Sapperton Tunnel**. Walk above the tunnel's portico to a field. Bear half right up to a stile. Cross to a path and walk up to a lane which leads back into **Sapperton**.

Weaving Along the Stroud Valley

Discover the impact of the Industrial Revolution in the steep-sided Cotswold valleys.

•DISTANCE•	6 miles (9.7km)
•MINIMUM TIME•	3hrs
•ASCENT / GRADIENT•	495ft (150m) ▲▲▲
•LEVEL OF DIFFICULTY•	梵 梵 梵
•PATHS•	Fields, lanes, canal path and tracks, 3 stiles
•LANDSCAPE•	Canal, road and railway, valley and steep slopes, villages
•SUGGESTED MAP•	aqua3 OS Explorer 168 Stroud, Tetbury and Malmesbury
•START / FINISH•	Grid reference: SO 892025
•DOG FRIENDLINESS•	Good, with few stiles and little livestock
•PARKING•	Lay-by east of Chalford church
•PUBLIC TOILETS•	None on route

BACKGROUND TO THE WALK

Wool has been associated with the Cotswolds for many centuries. During the Middle Ages the fleece of the 'Cotswold Lion' breed was the most prized in all of Europe. Merchants from many countries despatched their agents to purchase it from the fairs and markets of the wold towns in the northern part of the region – most famously Northleach, Cirencester and Chipping Campden. Woven cloth eventually became a more important export and so the industry moved to the southern Cotswolds, with its steeper valleys and faster-flowing streams, which were well suited to powering woollen mills.

Mechanisation

The concentration of mills in the Stroud area was evident by the early 15th century. Indeed, its importance was such that in a 1557 Act of Parliament that restricted cloth manufacture to towns, the villages of the Stroud area were exempted. By 1700 the lower Stroud Valley was producing 30,000 bolts (about 4.59 million sq m) of cloth every year. At this time the spinning and weaving was done in domestic dwellings or workhouses, the woven cloth then being returned to the mill for fulling, roughening and shearing. The mills were driven by the natural flow of the streams but the Industrial Revolution was to bring rapid change. There was great opposition to the introduction of mechanical spinning and shearing machines. This was heightened in 1795 by the development of the improved broadloom with its flying shuttle. The expectation was that, as well as compelling weavers to work in the mills rather that at home, it would bring mass unemployment. Progress marched on, however, and by the mid-19th century there were over 1,000 looms at work in the Stroud Valley. They came with their share of political unrest too, and in 1825 and 1828 strikes and riots had to be quelled by troops. The industry went into decline through the course of the 19th century, as steam replaced water power and it migrated northwards to the Pennines. By 1901 only 3,000 people were employed in the cloth industry, compared with 24,000 in the mid-17th century. Today, only one mill remains.

Graceful Elevations

This walk begins in Chalford, an attractive village built on the steep sides of the Stroud Valley. Its streets are lined with terraces of 18th- and 19th-century clothiers' houses and weavers' cottages. On the canalside the shells of woollen mills are still plentiful.

The 18th-century church contains fine examples of craftsmanship from the 'Arts and Crafts' period of the late 19th century. Nether Lypiatt Manor is a handsome manor house now owned by Prince and Princess Michael of Kent. Known locally as 'the haunted house', it was built in 1702 for Judge Charles Cox. Its classical features and estate railings, all unusual in the Cotswolds, inspired wealthy clothiers to spend their money on the addition of graceful elevations to their own houses.

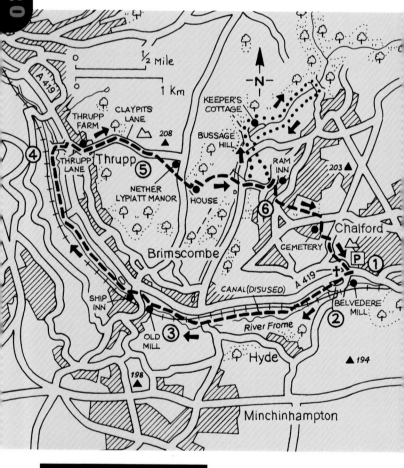

Walk 20 Directions

① Walk towards **Chalford church**. Immediately before it, cross the road and locate a path going right, towards a canal roundhouse. Note the **Belvedere Mill** across to your

left and follow the tow path alongside the **Thames and Severn Canal** on your right.

② Cross a road and continue along the tow path as it descends steps. Now follow this path for about 2 miles (3.2km). It will soon disappear under the railway line via a gloomy culvert, so that the **railway** will now be on your right, beyond the old canal. Old mills and small factories line the route.

③ Shortly before arriving in **Brimscombe** the path passes beneath the railway again. Soon after, it becomes a road leading into an industrial estate. At a road opposite a large, old mill turn left, to come to a junction. Cross and turn right. Immediately after the **Ship Inn** turn left along a road among offices and workshops. Continue straight on along a path, with factory walls to your right. The canal reappears on your left. As you walk on into the country you will pass beneath three brick bridges and a metal footbridge.

> **WHILE YOU'RE THERE** ⓘ
> High up on the far side of the Stroud Valley, there are a number of places to go. **Woodchester** has a well-preserved, Roman mosaic and an unfinished, 19th-century gothic mansion. **Rodborough Common** is the site of an 18th- and 19th-century fort that was originally built as a luxurious palace by a wealthy wool dyer. At **Selsley** is a little church filled with stained glass designed by members of the Arts and Crafts Movement.

④ At the next bridge, with a hamlet high on your left, turn right to follow a path to a road. Cross this and turn left. After a few paces turn right up a short path to meet **Thrupp Lane**. Turn right. At the top, turn left into **Claypits Lane**, turn right just before **Thrupp Farm** and climb up steeply.

> **WHAT TO LOOK FOR** ⓘ
> As you walk along the Stroudwater Canal look out for the **birds** that like to creep among the reeds: moorhens and coots, of course, but occasionally a heron will suddenly launch itself up from out of the undergrowth. Voles and stoats can be seen, and even the occasional adder.

⑤ After a long climb, as the road levels out, you will see **Nether Lypiatt Manor** in front of you. Turn right, beside a tree, over a stile into a field. Go half left to the far corner. Cross a stone stile and follow a narrow path beside trees to a road. Descend a lane opposite. Where it appears to fork, go straight on, to descend past a house. Enter **woodland** and fork right near the bottom. Keep a pond on your left and cross a road to climb **Bussage Hill**. After 100yds (91m) pass a lane on the left. At the top fork left. Opposite the **Ram Inn** turn right.

⑥ After a telephone box and bus shelter turn left to follow a path among houses into woodland. Go ahead until you meet a road. Turn left and immediately right down a path beside a **cemetery**. Descend to another road. Turn right for 50yds (46m), then turn left down a steep lane among trees, leading back to **Chalford**. At the bottom turn left to return to the start of the walk.

> **WHERE TO EAT AND DRINK** ⓘ
> There are two easy possibilities en route: the **Ship Inn** at Brimscombe and the **Ram Inn** at Bussage. Only a short distance from Brimscombe is Stroud, which has several restaurants and cafes.

Walk 21

Bird's-eye View of Abergavenny

A short sortie on to the hill that towers above the Beacons' eastern gateway.

•DISTANCE•	3 miles (4.8km)
•MINIMUM TIME•	1hr 30min
•ASCENT / GRADIENT•	530ft (161m) ▲▲▲
•LEVEL OF DIFFICULTY•	🚶 🚶 🚶
•PATHS•	Clear tracks over open mountainside, quiet lane, no stiles
•LANDSCAPE•	Rugged mountain scenery, huge views over Usk Valley
•SUGGESTED MAP•	aqua3 OS Explorer OL13 Brecon Beacons National Park Eastern area
•START / FINISH•	Grid reference: SO 270109
•DOG FRIENDLINESS•	Care needed near livestock
•PARKING•	Small car park at Carn-y-gorfydd
•PUBLIC TOILETS•	None on route

BACKGROUND TO THE WALK

There's no easier peak to climb in the Brecon Beacons National Park, but there are also few that occupy such a commanding position. The Blorenge – the English-sounding name probably derives from 'blue ridge'– towers menacingly above the cramped streets of Abergavenny, with the main sweep of the Black Mountains leading way to the north. The mountain actually dominates a small finger of the National Park that points southwards from Abergavenny to Pontypool. It's unique in being the only real peak south of the A465 Heads of the Valleys road. It also marks a watershed between the protected mountain scenery that makes up the bulk of the National Park and the ravaged industrial landscape that forms the southern boundary. Typically, its northern flanks boast a Bronze-Age burial cairn and the ground above the escarpment is littered with grass-covered mounds, a remnant of past quarrying. The stone was then transported away on the canals and railways.

Y Fenni

Commonly seen as the eastern gateway to the park, even if it sits just outside the boundary, Abergavenny is a thriving market town that owes its success to weaving, tanning and farming. It feels a thousand miles away from the industrial valleys that nudge against its limits from the south. The name, which in Welsh means the confluence of the River Venny, refers to its position at the junction of the River Fenni and the River Usk, but oddly, in Welsh, it's known simply as Y Fenni – the name of the river.

Norman Castle

Abergavenny sprang up around a Norman castle that was built to aid efforts by the invaders to rid the area of the Celts. The Welsh proved far more resilient than the Normans had expected and in the end, William de Braose, the lord of the town at the time, resorted to dirty tactics to achieve his aims, such as inviting the Welsh leaders to dinner and then murdering them while they were unarmed. The castle now acts as a museum with some interesting displays of the town's history. Another of Abergavenny's claims to fame is the fact that during World War Two, Hitler's deputy, Rudolf Hess, was imprisoned here after his plane crashed in Scotland.

Iron Town

Only 5 miles (8km) south of Abergavenny, but culturally and spiritually a completely different world, Blaenavon tells the full, uncut story of industrial expansion in South Wales. With iron ore, limestone, coal and water all found in local abundance, smelting began here as early as the 1500s, but the town, and the huge iron works that came to dominate it, didn't really get going until the Industrial Revolution of the late 18th century.

The colliery, now known as the Big Pit Mining Museum, was founded a full century later than the iron works and only closed as recently as 1980. It has been immaculately preserved and well organised to give visitors a meaningful insight into the industry itself, the conditions that the people endured and the culture that grew up around them. As well as the engine houses, workshops and the miners' baths, a tour, usually accompanied by a genuine ex-miner as a guide, includes donning a miner's helmet to descend one of the shafts to the actual coal-faces. Blaenavon is considered such an exceptional example of industrial South Wales that it was declared a UNESCO World Heritage Site in 2000.

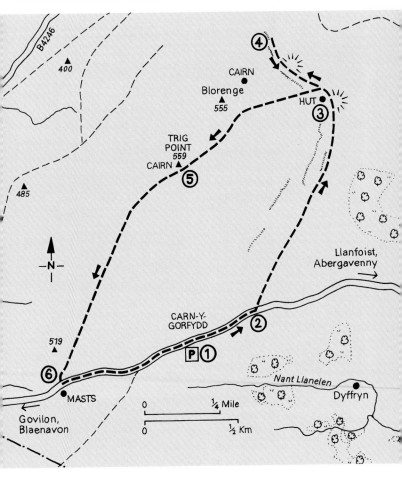

Walk 21

Walk 21 Directions

① From **Carn-y-gorfydd Roadside Rest**, walk downhill for 500yds (457m) and bear left, through a green barrier, on to a grassy track.

② This leads easily uphill, through a tangle of bracken, eventually allowing great views over the Usk Valley towards the outlying peak of Ysgyryd Fawr.

WHILE YOU'RE THERE ⓘ

Blaenavon is well worth visiting. As well as the iron works and Big Pit Mining Museum, there's also the incredibly scenic train ride along a short section of the Pontypool and Blaenavon Railway, the highest standard-gauge track in Wales today. It stops off at the Whistle Inn, a nostalgic miner's pub that would have once taken it's fair share of the modest wages paid to the men at the face.

---

③ As the path levels you'll pass a small **hut**. Continue along the escarpment edge, on one of a series of terraces that contour above the steep escarpment, and enjoy the views over Abergavenny and the Black Mountains. The rough ground was formed by the quarrying of stone.

④ Return to the hut and bear right, on to a clear, grassy track that climbs slightly and becomes stony. Away to the right, you should be able to make out the pronounced hump of a Bronze-Age burial cairn. The path now leads easily to the trig point and the huge **cairn** that mark the summit.

WHAT TO LOOK FOR ⓘ

This is one of the best places in South Wales to see and hear **red grouse**, which were once managed on these moors. The size of a pheasant, without the long tail, the male is a rusty reddish brown colour and the female more buff and mottled. You'll usually be alerted to their presence by a stabbing, alarmed clucking, followed by a short frantic escape flight.

---

⑤ Continue in the same direction, drop down past an impressive limestone outcrop and towards the huge **masts** on the skyline. You should also be able to see the extensive spoil heaps on the flanks of Gilwern Hill, directly ahead.

WHERE TO EAT AND DRINK ⓘ

There are a few good options in the area at the mountain's foot. The **Cordell Country Inn** above Govilon is well worth a visit, especially for the 2-course Sunday lunch, as is the **Llanfoist Inn** in Llanfoist village. There's also plenty of choice in Abergavenny town.

---

⑥ At the masts, you'll meet the road where you turn left and continue easily downhill, for 600yds (549m), back to the start.

Back to Purple

From the mining village of Snailbeach to the dragon's crest of Stiperstones.

•DISTANCE•	4½ miles (7.2km)
•MINIMUM TIME•	2hrs
•ASCENT / GRADIENT•	951ft (290m) ▲▲▲
•LEVEL OF DIFFICULTY•	👫 👫 👫
•PATHS•	Good paths across pasture, moorland and woodland, 1 stile
•LANDSCAPE•	Shropshire's second highest hill, with great views
•SUGGESTED MAP•	aqua3 OS Explorer 216 Welshpool & Montgomery
•START / FINISH•	Grid reference: SJ 373022
•DOG FRIENDLINESS•	On lead in nature reserve and near livestock
•PARKING•	Car park at Snailbeach
•PUBLIC TOILETS•	At car park

BACKGROUND TO THE WALK

At first sight it looks as though this walk will be all about industrial archaeology, for it begins at Snailbeach, formerly one of the most important lead mines in Britain. Mining ceased long ago and the derelict landscape has been transformed into one of the most fascinating post-industrial sites in the Midlands, complete with engine houses, loco sheds, compressors, crushers and tramways.

But there's another sort of transformation going on near by, on the rugged moorland ridge of Stiperstones. This is the Back to Purple project which aims to restore Stiperstones to its full glory. The quartzite ridge was formed 480 million years ago. During the last ice age it stood out above the glaciers and was subjected to constant freezing and thawing, which shattered much of the quartzite into a mass of scree surrounding several residual tors and leaving the top of the ridge jagged as a dragon's or dinosaur's crest. Subsequent soil formation has been so slow that much of the scree remains on the surface, largely unvegetated. Where soil has formed, it is thin, acidic and nutrient-poor, sufficient only to support a limited range of plants. Over much of the summit area the vegetation is dominated by heather and whinberry, with some crowberry and cowberry. At one time, this meant that in summer most of Stiperstones, except the very crest, turned a glorious purple.

Part of Stiperstones is protected, but modern agriculture and silviculture have encroached, fragmenting the ridge with areas of improved grassland and conifers so that it no longer turns nearly so purple. But things are changing. For several years it has been the subject of the ambitious Back to Purple initiative, managed by a partnership of English Nature, Forest Enterprise and Shropshire Wildlife Trust. Thousands of conifers have been felled, including the unsightly Gatten Plantation, which lay just below the summit ridge (and is still shown on OS maps). On the southern part of the ridge, further conifers have been cleared to reveal the jagged outline of Nipstone Rock, hidden for many years. Thousands of heather seedlings have been planted in these areas to supplement natural regeneration.

Work is also being undertaken to restore and protect other habitats which lie below the summit ridge such as herb-rich grasslands, hay meadows, wet flushes and woodland. The flora of these areas includes bog cotton, heath bedstraw and the increasingly scarce mountain pansy.

Walk 22 **Directions**

① Take the **Lordshill lane** opposite the car park, then join a parallel footpath on the left. Rejoining the lane, cross to the site of the locomotive shed, then continue up the lane, noticing the green arrows directing you to the main sites.

② Turn right on a track between the **crusher house** and the **compressor house**. A few paces past the compressor house, turn left up steps. At the top, turn right, then soon left up more steps. Turn left to the Cornish engine house, then right and continue through woodland. A short detour leads to the smelter chimney, otherwise it's uphill all the way.

WHERE TO EAT AND DRINK ⓘ
There is nothing along the way, but you are not far from the **Stiperstones Inn**, open for food and drink from 8 in the morning until 10 at night. It also acts as a tourist information point, sells maps and walks leaflets and offers B&B. Dogs are allowed in the bar, but not the lounge bar. There are also shops and pubs in **Minsterley**, north of Snailbeach.

③ A sign indicates that you're entering **Stiperstones National Nature Reserve** (NNR). The woods give way to bracken, broom and bramble before you cross a stile to the open hill. A path climbs the slope ahead to a stile/gate at the top.

④ Two paths are waymarked. Take the left-hand one, which runs between a fence and the rim of the spectacular dingle on your right. The path then climbs away from the dingle and meets a rutted track. Turn right. As the path climbs you can see the rock tors on the

summit. There's also one much closer to hand, isolated from the rest. This is **Shepherd's Rock**.

⑤ Just beyond Shepherd's Rock is a junction marked by a cairn. Turn right here, then fork left to go round the other side of the rock. Leave the NNR at a gate/stile. The path runs to the left, shortly bordered by a hawthorn hedge. You'll soon see that this is an old green lane, lined at various points by either hedges/trees on both sides, one line of trees or a tumbledown stone wall.

WHILE YOU'RE THERE ⓘ
Explore the Snailbeach site, then visit The Bog Mine, a little further south. There's a seasonal visitor centre, waymarked walks and mine workings. Be there at dusk if you'd like to see some bats – they live in one of the mine tunnels (known as The Somme) which has been blocked by a grid for their protection.

⑥ At a junction take the left-hand path back into the NNR. At the next junction, fork right to leave the NNR at a gate by a plantation. Go diagonally across a field to a track; turn right, going back across the field, through the plantation, then across pasture on a bridleway.

⑦ Fork left at a bridleway junction and continue past **Lordshill chapel** to a lane. Turn right and stay with it as it swings left to **Snailbeach**.

WHAT TO LOOK FOR ⓘ
Lordshill Baptist chapel, built in 1833 and enlarged in 1873, was in regular use until recently. After a period of disuse it was restored and Sunday meetings are held here most summers. It also appeared in the film of Mary Webb's *Gone to Earth*, which was set on Stiperstones.

Highley Enterprising and Enjoyable

Trace the history of Highley's miners on a Severn Valley sculpture trail.

•DISTANCE•	5½ miles (8.8km)
•MINIMUM TIME•	2hrs 30min
•ASCENT / GRADIENT•	490ft (150m) ▲ ▲ ▲
•LEVEL OF DIFFICULTY•	🚶 🚶 🚶
•PATHS•	Woodland, pasture and riverside tow path, 16 stiles
•LANDSCAPE•	Two wooded valleys and ridge between
•SUGGESTED MAP•	aqua3 OS Explorer 218 Wyre Forest & Kidderminster
•START / FINISH•	Grid reference: SO 745830
•DOG FRIENDLINESS•	On leads along east side of Borle Brook, in pastureland near Whitehouse Farm and in Highley churchyard
•PARKING•	Severn Valley Country Park, Station Road, Highley
•PUBLIC TOILETS•	At car park

BACKGROUND TO THE WALK

The first thing to say about this walk is yes, it is a weird shape! That's purely because of the appalling state of some of the other local footpaths, but don't let that put you off. The paths on this route are fine and it's an excellent walk in beautiful countryside.

Victorian Town

You don't expect to find mining towns in Shropshire, but Highley is one, albeit in miniature. An ex-mining town, to be precise, but if that conjures up a depressing image, Highley confounds expectation again. Its terraces of well-built, well-preserved and obviously well-loved Victorian houses are trim, attractive and harmonious, their period features mostly intact and their gable walls and window sills all painted bright red in an idiosyncratic touch which may sound disastrous, but actually works perfectly. The Victorian (or possibly Victorian-style) street signs are charming too.

Mines and Quarries

Quarrying was important here long before mining – some of the stone for Worcester Cathedral came from Highley. Although coal mining began in the Middle Ages, large-scale operations commenced only in 1878, peaking in the 1930s. Highley Mining Company also opened collieries at Kinlet and Billingsley. Most of the coal dug at Highley went down a tramway to Highley Station on the Severn Valley Railway (SVR). The tramway is now a footpath, which you'll follow on this walk. Tramways and railways were built to link the other mines to the SVR as well. Billingsley Colliery Railway ran along the west bank of Borle Brook, joining the SVR at Brooksmouth. A tramway ran along the east bank and both are now footpaths, also used in this walk.

If you've done homework you'll know that the mines closed in 1969 and the former industrial areas on both sides of the river have been transformed into a country park. Highley has also gone in for some public artwork, including a sculpture trail, known as the

Seam Pavement Trail, by West Midlands artist Saranjit Birdi. This is a series of seven bronze plaques depicting Highley's past. The imaginative designs incorporate miners' nicknames gleaned from archive information and consultation with locals. The names, including such gems as Dick the Devil, Flaming Heck and Joyful Clappers, were passed down through the generations, forming what Saranjit calls a seam through time. The plaques are terrific, with possibly the most striking being *Trail Boss*, *Name Poem* and *Plough and Lady*. The latter depicts Lady Godiva (of Coventry fame), who owned Highley Manor in the 11th century. Saranjit Birdi is also responsible for the sculpture *A Song of Steam Trains* at Highley Station.

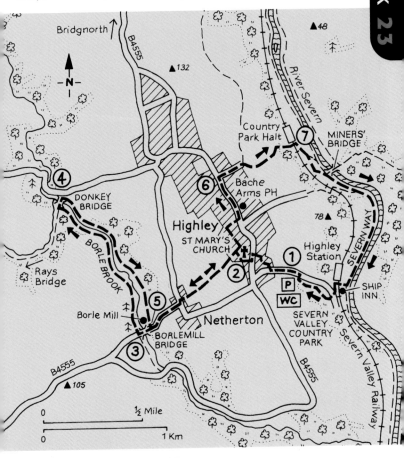

Walk 23 **Directions**

① Turn left up **Station Road**. When you're almost at the top, turn right at a sign for the Seam Pavement Trail. Follow a footpath (**Smoke Alley**) to the main road. Turn left, then cross to a footpath to **St Mary's Church**.

② Go through the churchyard of St Mary's, leaving it by the side of timber-framed **Church House**. Make your way down a stony track, then pass to the left of **Springfield**, on a public footpath which runs along field edges to reach a lane. Walk down another lane almost opposite, which is signposted 'Borle Mill and Kinlet'.

Walk 23

③ Cross **Borlemill Bridge** and turn right on a public footpath. It's hidden among conifers, but it's opposite an easily seen path on the other side. After passing a house, continue along field edges and then through the woodland which borders **Borle Brook**.

④ The path arrives at **Donkey Bridge** (an 18th-century packhorse bridge), which you will need to cross. Before you do so, however, it's worth going a few paces to the left to see an old railway bridge. (If you're keen to trace the Billingsley Colliery Railway as far as you can, you should turn left on a bridleway which goes to Rays Bridge, but you'll have to return the same way, owing to the impassability of other footpaths). Having crossed Donkey Bridge, turn right to walk back along the other side of **Borle Brook**. Don't

walk by the brook itself, instead take a higher path, through woods and meadows.

⑤ Turn left when you come to the lane and retrace your steps to **Highley**. Pass to the left of the church and left again on **Church Street**. Follow it to **High Street** (again watching for the pavement trail plaques) and turn left.

⑥ Turn right on **Vicarage Lane**, which will take you past four 400-year-old pollarded beeches, known locally as the Seven Sisters (some say there were once seven trees, others say it's Severn Sisters), to a junction where you fork right over a cattle grid. The track descends to four gates. Go through the one on the right.

⑦ Cross the railway by **Country Park Halt** and turn right, passing through woodland. At a junction with a surfaced track, turn left to **Miners' Bridge**, then join the Severn Way, signposted to Highley Station. When you reach the **Ship Inn**, built for bargemen and opened in 1770, another signpost directs you to Highley Station. Cross the line, then turn left until you come to a path climbing through woods. This is the former tramway and it goes directly up taking you back to the car park.

Exploring Shropshire's China Town

Woodland, the River Severn and fascinating industrial remains make for a superb walk in Ironbridge Gorge.

Walk 24

•DISTANCE•	5 miles (8km)
•MINIMUM TIME•	2hrs
•ASCENT / GRADIENT•	295ft (90m) ▲▲▲
•LEVEL OF DIFFICULTY•	🚶 🚶🚶 🚶🚶
•PATHS•	Mostly excellent, though path through Lee Dingle is quite rough and may be muddy, 1 stile
•LANDSCAPE•	Woodland and riverbank
•SUGGESTED MAP•	aqua3 OS Explorer 242 Telford, Ironbridge & The Wrekin
•START / FINISH•	Grid reference: SJ 677033
•DOG FRIENDLINESS•	No sheep or cattle so can run fairly freely
•PARKING•	Next to Bedlam Furnaces on Waterloo Street, between Ironbridge and Jackfield Bridge
•PUBLIC TOILETS•	At Ironbridge end of Waterloo Street

BACKGROUND TO THE WALK

Coalport china is famous the world over, and rightly so, for it's exquisite stuff. The story of how it came to be made here is interesting too. Coalport, which is much smaller today than it was at its peak, was planned as a canal-river interchange and a complete new town by ironmaster William Reynolds. Between 1788 and 1796 he built warehouses, workshops, factories and cottages on formerly undeveloped land by the river. Crucially, he also constructed the Shropshire Canal to link the East Shropshire Coalfield with the River Severn. The terminus was at Coalport Wharf, between the Brewery Inn and Coalport Bridge.

Monument to Industry

The canal greatly aided the new town's development, especially after the completion of the Hay Inclined Plane in 1793. This is one of the country's major industrial monuments, the best preserved and most spectacular of its kind. It was the means by which boats were transferred from the top to the bottom of the gorge. Equivalent to 27 locks, but worked by only four men, it could pass six boats in an hour, a feat which would have taken three hours using a lock system. The boats were carried up and down the almost 1 in 4 gradient on wheeled cradles. The incline is now part of Blists Hill Museum, but you can see part of it on this walk. After the canal was superseded by a railway it silted up, became overgrown and was infilled during the 1920s. It was partially restored in 1976 and again in the 1990s.

In 1795 the Coalport China Company was founded by John Rose in the large building which is now a youth hostel and café. Across the former canal is a later china works, now Coalport China Museum, showing factory life and manufacturing techniques. Even if you don't go inside the museum, the whole site, with mellow brick buildings and enormous kilns, is wonderfully evocative. China manufacture ceased here in 1926 when the company moved to the Potteries. Coalport China is now part of the Wedgwood group.

Walk 24

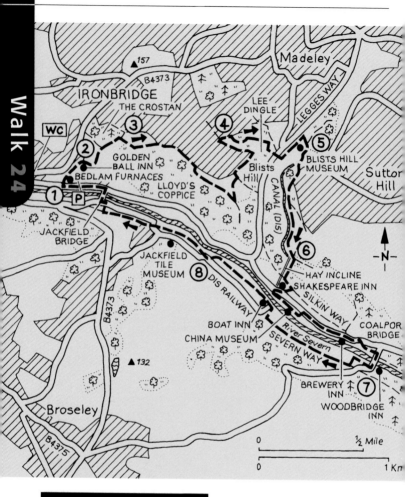

① To the left of the furnaces (as you stand facing them) a path climbs into parkland, then zig-zags up through a succession of wisteria-covered pergolas and flights of steps. Turn right at the top, then left on **Newbridge Road** to a junction.

② Pass to the left of the **Golden Ball Inn**, then turn right at the junction with Jockey Bank, past **Victoria Cottage**. Go left at another junction and through a gate into a wood called **The Crostan**. A stepped path climbs to a junction

where two paths are indicated. Take the right-hand one, climbing by the woodland edge to another waymarked junction.

③ Turn right on a bridleway, which runs across two meadows into woodland. Continue through the wood, with **Lloyd's Coppice** clinging to the steep slope on your right. Fork left at two junctions; at the second one the bridleway leaves the trees to continue between woodland and houses.

④ A stile on the right gives access to **Lee Dingle**, where a path descends towards the road. Cross

Legges Way, turn left under two bridges, then soon right on a footpath by the entrance to **Blists Hill Museum**.

⑤ Ignore a path branching left and carry straight on past a line of wooden posts. Turn right on a footpath by the last post, skirting the Blists Hill site and soon entering woodland. Ignore paths branching left and keep close to the museum site. Soon you'll see the canal through the trees. When the path enters grassland, it forks; keep left, with trees between the path and the canal. At the next junction turn right, glimpsing the top of the great **Hay Incline**.

> ### WHILE YOU'RE THERE ℹ
> **Blists Hill Museum** re-creates the sights, sounds and smells of a late Victorian town. The staff wear period costume and you can exchange your money at the bank for Victorian coinage to spend in the shops or pub. Watch someone mucking out a pigsty, operating a steam engine or pouring iron in a foundry, or learn about the scary side of Victorian medicine in the chemist's shop.

⑥ Following signs for Coalport, descend to a junction by a bridge. Turn left on the **Silkin Way**, then immediately right and right again past the **Shakespeare Inn** and **Tunnel Tea Rooms**. Cross a road bridge, then turn left across the **Shropshire Canal** and left again on the tow path. Re-cross the canal at the next footbridge and walk past the **China Museum**, Coalport Youth Hostel and Slip Room Café. Join Coalport **High Street** and continue in the same direction, rejoining the **Silkin Way** opposite the **Brewery Inn**. Follow the track to **Coalport Bridge**, then cross over the river.

> ### WHERE TO EAT AND DRINK ℹ
> There are numerous possibilities mentioned in the route description. All look appealing, most allow dogs and several offer children's menus and vegetarian choices. The **Boat Inn** is particularly interesting, with its mural of a Severn trow (flat-bottomed, square-sailed trading vessel), and past flood levels marked on the door. It has a garden and riverside tables, as do the **Brewery Inn** and the **Woodbridge Inn**. The museums and craft centre all have cafés.

⑦ Turn right on the Severn Way, which passes through **Preen's Eddy** picnic area, then climbs away from the river to continue along a former railway trackbed. Turn right at signs for Silkin Way via Jackfield Bridge and you'll come to the **Boat Inn**. Head towards Ironbridge past lovely cottages and **Maws Craft Centre**.

⑧ As you approach a black-and-white-painted former pub, a path takes you on to its access track, bending left into woodland. Turn right towards Ironbridge, soon joining **Church Road**. Pass **Jackfield Tile Museum** and the Calcutts House, then carry straight on at **Jackfield Sidings**, passing the **Black Swan**. When a bridge crosses the path you can access the river. Cross **Jackfield Bridge**, then turn left past the **Robin Hood Inn** and the **Bird in Hand** to return to **Bedlam Furnaces**.

> ### WHAT TO LOOK FOR ℹ
> **Bedlam Furnaces** were built in 1757 by the Madeley Wood Furnace Company and taken over by William Reynolds in 1794. They were used to smelt iron ore and are blast furnaces similar to those developed by Abraham Darby I. If a blast furnace was allowed to cool its lining would crack, so smelting was continuous, with employees working 12-hour shifts.

Revolution at Coalbrookdale

An absorbing walk in the wooded hills and valleys where the Industrial Revolution began.

•DISTANCE•	5 miles (8km)
•MINIMUM TIME•	2hrs
•ASCENT / GRADIENT•	770ft (235m) ▲▲ ▲ ▲
•LEVEL OF DIFFICULTY•	🚶🚶 🚶🚶 🚶
•PATHS•	Woodland paths, lots of steps (mostly descending), may be fallen trees at Strethill, 2 stiles, some paths very overgrown
•LANDSCAPE•	Wooded hills of Severn Gorge
•SUGGESTED MAP•	aqua3 OS Explorer 242 Telford, Ironbridge & The Wrekin
•START / FINISH•	Grid reference: SJ 664037
•DOG FRIENDLINESS•	Excellent, but keep under strict control at Strethill (sheep)
•PARKING•	Dale End Riverside Park, just west of Museum of the Gorge
•PUBLIC TOILETS•	In Museum of the Gorge car park

BACKGROUND TO THE WALK

People have been smelting iron for many centuries, but production was originally small scale because smelting was dependent on timber which first had to be made into charcoal – a slow and laborious process. All that changed at Coalbrookdale in 1709 when Abraham Darby I perfected a method of smelting iron with coke instead of charcoal. It may sound a small thing, but it sparked a revolution that changed the world. At long last iron could be made cheaply in large quantities and it came to be increasingly used in many areas of engineering.

World Leader

By 1785 the Coalbrookdale district had become the foremost industrial area in the world. It was particularly celebrated for its innovations: the first iron bridge, the first iron boat, the first iron rails and the first steam locomotive. Tourists came from far and wide to see the sights, and artists came to paint it all – furnaces lighting up the night sky was a favourite subject. Decline eventually set in due to competition from the Black Country and South Wales and the area fell into decay. Since the 1960s, the surviving industrial relics have been transformed into a fascinating collection of museums and the gorge has been designated a UNESCO World Heritage Site. Perhaps even more remarkable than the industrial heritage is the way nature has reclaimed sites of industrial despoilation and made them beautiful again. These regenerated woods and meadows are managed by the Severn Gorge Countryside Trust and are accessible to the public.

Taking Care of the Workers

The ironmasters were paternalistic types who built decent houses for their workers and took an interest in their moral well-being. When you walk through Dale Coppice and Lincoln Hill Woods you will be using the Sabbath Walks, designed by Richard Reynolds to provide healthy Sunday recreation for his workers. The idea was that this would keep them from drinking, gambling and sexual promiscuity. A rotunda was erected at one viewpoint, but has since been demolished, though you can still enjoy the view. It's mostly woodland now, but you will see the remains of a great quarry that bit deep into Lincoln Hill. It extends so far underground that tours of its limestone caverns were popular with 19th-century day-trippers. Bands played in the illuminated caverns and thousands came on excursion trains from the Black Country and Birmingham.

Walk 25 **Directions**

① Follow the **River Severn** upstream, using the Severn Way, and pass under two bridges. After the second one, bear away from the river towards **Buildwas Road**. At the road, turn left for a few paces, then cross to a footpath that ascends through woodland. Keep close to the edge until a waymarker directs you obliquely right.

② Cross a stile and continue in the same direction over pastureland. Pass under a pylon, then join a farm track and turn left through a gate. Follow the hawthorn hedge on your right to a junction, turn left on a bridleway and follow it along field edges, then across the middle of a meadow to a lane. Turn left.

③ Leave the lane when it bridges a road, turning right on a farm access track (Shropshire Way). Go through a gate on the right, just before **Leasows Farm**, then downfield to enter **Lydebrook Dingle**. A path descends through the wood, beyond which you continue along a path called **Rope Walk**.

④ Descend some steps on the left into **Loamhole Dingle**. Cross **Loamhole Brook** at a footbridge and climb steps on the other side to a T-junction. Turn right on what is mostly boardwalk and, when you reach **Upper Furnace Pool**, cross it on a footbridge to meet the road.

⑤ Your onward route is to the left, but a short detour right leads to the **Darby Houses**, Tea Kettle Row and the Quaker Burial Ground. Resuming the walk, go down to **Darby Road** and turn right beside the viaduct and the **Museum of Iron**. Turn left under the viaduct at a junction with **Coach Road**. Follow the road past the museum and Coalbrookdale Works to a junction.

> **WHILE YOU'RE THERE** ⓘ
> The **Museum of Iron** brings the Darbys' achievements to life. It includes the Darby Furnace where it all began and it has much to say about the lives of those who lived and worked in the area during this period of momentous change. Equally fascinating are the ironmasters' homes near by (known as the **Darby Houses**) and the charming terrace of workers' houses at Tea Kettle Row.

⑥ Cross to **Church Road**, turn left after the Wesleyan chapel on the corner and enter **Dale Coppice**. Follow signs for Church Road at the first two junctions, but at the third ignore the Church Road sign and keep straight on. Leave the wood to enter grassland and go forward a few paces to meet a track. Turn left, then shortly fork right, staying on

> **WHERE TO EAT AND DRINK** ⓘ
> There is lots of choice, such as the **Swan**, a very attractive place which is open all day. Well-behaved dogs and children are welcome in the bar area, but no dogs where food is served. There's a special children's menu. Almost next door (the other side of Lincoln Hill limekilns), the **Malthouse** is equally attractive and also welcomes children, and dogs in the bar or outside.

the track. Go left at another junction, then right at the next two. Dale Coppice is on your right, a cemetery on your left.

⑦ A gate accesses **Dale Coppice**. Turn right, then soon left, going downhill to a junction marked by a bench. Turn right, then left when a sign indicates Church Road, and left again beside the road.

⑧ Turn right into **Lincoln Hill Wood** and follow signs for the Rotunda, soon arriving at a viewpoint where the Rotunda formerly stood. Descend a very steep flight of steps to a junction. Turn right, then left down more steps and left again, signposted to Lincoln Hill Road. Cross the road to a footpath opposite, that descends to the **Wharfage**. Turn right past Lincoln Hill lime kilns and the **Swan** to **Dale End Riverside Park**.

> **WHAT TO LOOK FOR** ⓘ
> Upper Furnace Pool in Loamhole Dingle is the pool that powered the bellows that blew the furnace where Abraham Darby first smelted iron with coke. The area of open water has been reduced by a profuse growth of **marsh horsetail**. This primeval-looking species is the evolutionary successor to the giant tree-like horsetails that were a major element in the swamp vegetation that 300 million years ago formed the coal measures.

From Castle to Canal

Follow the Llangollen branch of the Shroppie through pastoral countryside.

•DISTANCE•	6 miles (9.7km)
•MINIMUM TIME•	2hrs 30min
•ASCENT / GRADIENT•	Negligible
•LEVEL OF DIFFICULTY•	
•PATHS•	Tow path, lanes and field paths, very overgrown, 19 stiles
•LANDSCAPE•	Low-lying farmland, pastoral and arable, attractive canal
•SUGGESTED MAP•	aqua3 OS Explorer 240 Oswestry
•START / FINISH•	Grid reference: SJ 325312
•DOG FRIENDLINESS•	Can run free on tow path, but probably nowhere else
•PARKING•	Car park next to Whittington Castle – honesty box
•PUBLIC TOILETS•	At castle when open

BACKGROUND TO THE WALK

This walk explore sections of the Montgomery Canal (the Monty). Read about the history of it here, then learn about recent restoration work. The waterway that we now call the Montgomery Canal runs for 35 miles (56km) from the Llangollen (formerly Ellesmere) Canal at Frankton Junction to Newtown, Powys. Originally, it was three canals – the Ellesmere, and the eastern and western branches of the Montgomery – built by three different companies over 25 years. The Ellesmere (Frankton to Llanymynech) section opened first, in 1796. It met the Montgomery Canal's eastern branch at Carreghofa, but the Monty was completed only as far as Garthmyl (near Welshpool) before the money ran out in 1797. Work ceased for years until a Newtown entrepreneur, William Pugh, put up the cash. By 1819 it was finally finished, right through to Newtown.

A Long Time Coming

Frankton Junction became the hub of the Ellesmere system. There were actually two junctions, forming an H-shape, from which waterways radiated out to Weston Lullingfields, Ellesmere, Pontcysyllte and Llanymynech. The limestone quarries at Llanymynech provided one of the canal's most valuable cargoes. The Weston branch was intended to continue to Shrewsbury, but was never completed. It's derelict today.

Many renowned engineers were involved with the Monty, including father-and-son teams William and Josias Jessop and John and Thomas Dadford, as well as Thomas Telford. In engineering terms it's an unusual canal; it first descends by 11 locks from Frankton to the Severn, then climbs again, with 14 locks taking it up the Severn Valley to Newtown.

By 1850, the Monty had become part of the Shropshire Union Railway and Canal Company (the Shroppie), but was subsequently taken over by the London and North Western Railway Company. In 1923, it came into the ownership of the London, Midland and Scottish Railway Company (LMS). In 1936, the canal burst its banks by the River Perry below Frankton Locks. The LMS made no effort to repair it; the canal was simply left to its fate. Legal abandonment came in 1944 with the LMS Act of Parliament, which closed many miles of waterway. Under the 1948 Transport Act, the Monty passed into the ownership of British Waterways. Restoration work began in 1968.

0   ½ Mile

0   1 Km

FRANKTON
LOCKS

LOCKGATE
BRIDGE

Montgomery
Canal

▲153

Welsh
Frankton

▲88

Berghill

A495

LLANGOLLEN CANAL

Marina

③

Narrowboat
Inn

▲110

Perry
Farm

POLLETT'S
BRIDGE

④

River Perry

Big Wood

Halston
Gardens

Halston
Hall

②

HINDFORD
BRIDGE

Hindford

JACK
MYTTON
INN

⑤

DISMANTLED RAILWAY

A495

Ye Olde
Boote
PH

B5009

White
Lion PH

Fern
Lees

⑥

105 ▲

P CASTLE

①

Whittington

River Perry

B5009

A495

Gobowen

Oswestry

Walk 26 **Directions**

① Turn right by the Shrewsbury road (**B5009**), using a footway on the left. After about ½ mile (800m), cross a stile and follow a waymarked path across three fields to the far right corner of the third.

② Walk along the edge of the next field, with a wood on your left. Cross a stile in the corner, then go obliquely across another field as indicated by a waymarker. A prominent oak tree is a useful guide. There is a stile near the tree, but you may have to wade through nettles to get to it. Continue in the same direction across the next field to a lane and turn left.

> ### WHAT TO LOOK FOR
> The village of Whittington is dominated by its 13th-century **castle**, built by Fulke FitzWarine on the site of an earlier timber castle. What remains of his stronghold is mostly earthworks because the castle fell into disuse after the Civil War and its stone was plundered for road repairs. However, the handsome gatehouse survives intact, its twin circular towers reflected in the moat.

③ Keep left when you come to a fork and continue to the **A495**. Turn right for a few paces, then cross to the other side. Join a footpath that runs along the left-hand edge of a field to a stile and footbridge. Beyond these, keep going along the field edge until a gap in the hedge. Go through, but continue in the same direction as before, soon going up a bank.

④ Meet the canal at **Pollett's Bridge** (No 6). Don't cross it – go under to join the tow path. Follow this to **Hindford Bridge** (No 11), then go up to a lane. Turn right past the **Jack Mytton Inn**, then right again, signposted 'Iron Mills and Gobowen'.

> ### WHILE YOU'RE THERE
> Oswestry was once the headquarters of the Cambrian Railway and a hub for services to North Wales. One of the former engine sheds now houses the **Cambrian Museum of Transport**, which chronicles Oswestry's railway history. The Cambrian Railway Society regularly steams up one of its locos on site and there is plenty of railway memorabilia.

⑤ Take a footpath on the left. Walk down a long, narrow paddock to the far end, then cross a stile on the right. Follow a fence to a footbridge, then continue across the next pasture to another footbridge and keep straight on to a stile ahead. Go up to the far right corner of the next field, through a gate and then left by a field edge.

> ### WHERE TO EAT AND DRINK
> There is a **tea room** at the castle, a **Spar** shop near by and two pubs, **Ye Olde Boote** and the **White Lion**. The **Jack Mytton Inn** at Hindford is an appealing place with a large canalside garden in a very pleasant location. Children are welcome and there is a vegetarian menu.

⑥ Join a track that soon bends right beside the course of a dismantled railway. Look out for a stile giving access to the railway. Turn right on the former trackbed for a few paces, then up the bank on the left – watch out for steps concealed in the undergrowth here. Cross a stile to a field, turn right to the far side and cross another stile. Bear left to a large oak tree, then continue to a lane. Follow it to **Top Street** and turn right, then left to **Whittington Castle**.

Walk 27

There's Copper in Them There Hills

A walk up to the old copper mines of Mynydd Sygyn and through the spectacular Pass of Aberglaslyn.

•DISTANCE•	4 miles (6.4km)
•MINIMUM TIME•	2hrs 30min
•ASCENT / GRADIENT•	1,181ft (360m) ▲▲▲
•LEVEL OF DIFFICULTY•	𝍖 𝍖 𝍖
•PATHS•	Well-maintained paths and tracks (see note below), 2 stiles
•LANDSCAPE•	Rocky hills
•SUGGESTED MAP•	aqua3 OS Explorer OL17 Snowdon
•START / FINISH•	Grid reference: SH 597462
•DOG FRIENDLINESS•	Dogs should be on leads at all times
•PARKING•	National Trust pay car park, Aberglaslyn
•PUBLIC TOILETS•	At car park
•NOTE•	Short section of riverside path in Aberglaslyn gorge is difficult and requires use of handholds

BACKGROUND TO THE WALK

This route heads for the rugged hills forming one side of the great Aberglaslyn gorge that has graced many a postcard and book jacket. At the back of the car park you pass under a railway bridge that belonged to the Welsh Highland Railway and pass the site of an old crushing plant. Here, copper ore from the mountain would have been prepared for shipment, using the railway.

Cwm Bychan

Beyond the plant, the path follows a playful stream and climbs steadily through the lonely Cwm Bychan. Here, beneath splintered, craggy mountains patched with heather and bracken, you come across a line of rusting gantries. They're part of an old aerial ropeway, built to carry ore down to the crushing mill. Mining had taken place hereabouts since Roman times, but after World War One the extraction became uneconomical. In 1922 the mines closed.

Continuing to the col above, the route comes to a huge area of mining spoil and a meeting of routes. Ours turns south, and soon we're following a rugged rocky path zig-zagging down to a grassy basin below before continuing along a craggy ridge. Here the ground drops away steeply into the valley of the Afon Glaslyn. If it's early summer the scene will be emblazoned by the vivid pink blooms of rhododendrons, which smother the hillside. Hundreds of feet below lie the roof tops of Beddgelert and what lies in between is a glorious little path twisting through those rhododendrons and the rocks into the village. If you get that feeling of déjà vu the hillsides around here were used for the setting of the Chinese village in *The Inn of the Sixth Happiness* (1958), starring Igrid Bergman.

Beddgelert is a pretty village with a fine two-arched bridge spanning the Glaslyn and a handful of busy craft shops and cafés, which throng with visitors in the summer. Around here they're all too fond of telling you the story of Prince Llewelyn's brave dog, Gelert, and pointing to the grave which gave the village its name. Don't be misled; a past landlord of the Royal Goat devised the plausible story to boost his trade. We're going to head for the great gorge of Aberglaslyn!

The Gorge

The way back to Aberglaslyn used to be by way of the old Welsh Highland Railway trackbed, but the tunnels have been deemed unsafe and, halfway along the route, you're now forced to take a rough track by the raging river. The hard bit with handholds comes right at the beginning. If you can manage that you can enjoy the excitement of a walk through the gorge and through the attractive woodland that shades its banks. If you want to see that postcard view though, you'll have to make a short detour to the roadside at Pont Aberglaslyn. It's stunning if you haven't seen it before.

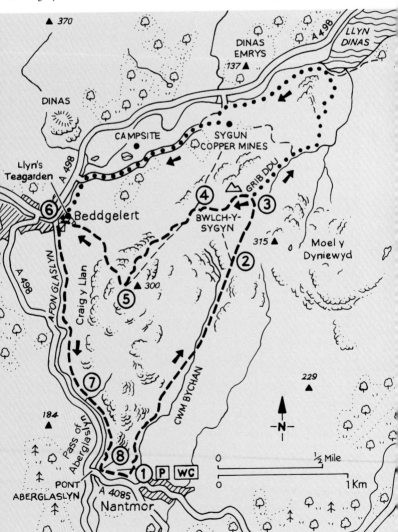

Walk 27

Walk 27 Directions

① The path starts to the left of the toilet block and goes under the old railway bridge, before climbing through **Cwm Bychan**. After a short climb the path continues past the iron pylons of the aerial cableway.

② Beyond the pylons, keep to the right of the cwm, ignoring paths forking left. A grassy corridor leads to a col, where there's a stile in a fence that is not shown on current maps. Turn left beyond the stile and head for a three-way footpath signpost by the rocks of **Grib Ddu**.

③ Follow the path on the left signed 'To Beddgelert and Sygun' and go over another ladder stile. After veering left, around a small rocky knoll, the path winds steeply down the hillside to the cairn at **Bwlch-y-Sygyn**. Here you'll see a shallow peaty pool in a green hollow to the left.

④ The path now heads south west along the mountain's north western 'edge', overlooking Beddgelert. Take the left fork to pass another signpost, where you should follow the 'Beddgelert' direction.

⑤ Watch out for a large cairn, highlighting the turn-off right for Beddgelert. The clear stony path weaves through rhododendron and rock, goes through a kissing gate in a wall half-way down, then descends further to the edge of

Beddgelert, where a little lane passing the cottage of **Penlan** leads to the **Afon Glaslyn**.

⑥ Turn left to follow the river for a short way. Don't cross the footbridge over the river but turn left through a kissing gate to follow the Glaslyn's east bank. The path joins and follows the trackbed of the old **Welsh Highland Railway**.

WHAT TO LOOK FOR ⓘ

The name Aberglaslyn at the start of the walk conjures up images of an estuary flowing into the sea, but here is a flat inland plain. The waves used to lap against these shores, but that was before the speculator William Maddocks persuaded the government of the day to build a land reclamation scheme. The **Cob**, across the southern end of the estuary allowed the land behind it to silt up and be cultivated.

---

⑦ Just before the first tunnel descend right to follow a rough path down to the river. Handholds screwed into the rocks allow passage on a difficult but short section. The path continues through riverside woodland and over boulders until it comes to **Pont Aberglaslyn**.

⑧ Here, turn left up some steps and follow a dirt path through the woods. After crossing the railway trackbed turn right, then right again to go under the old railway bridge back to the car park.

WHERE TO EAT AND DRINK ⓘ

If its lunchtime and you're halfway along the walk, try **Llyn's Teagarden and café** by the river in Beddgelert. They have a splendid riverside terrace for alfresco eating and serve a wide range of meals.

WHILE YOU'RE THERE ⓘ

If you have time, visit the **Sygun Copper Mines** to the North of Beddgelert. It's well worth taking one of their self-guided audio-visual tours. You'll go on foot around the winding tunnels and see the veins of copper ore in chambers coloured by a fascinating array of stalactites and stalagmites.

Snowdon the Long Way

A route that takes its time on one of Snowdon's seldom-trod ridges.

•DISTANCE•	10 miles (16.1km)
•MINIMUM TIME•	6hrs 30min
•ASCENT / GRADIENT•	3,839ft (1,170m) ▲ ▲ ▲
•LEVEL OF DIFFICULTY•	🚶 🚶 🚶
•PATHS•	Well-defined paths and tracks
•LANDSCAPE•	High mountain cwms and tarns
•SUGGESTED MAP•	aqua3 OS Explorer OL17 Snowdon
•START / FINISH•	Grid reference: SH 577604
•DOG FRIENDLINESS•	Can be let off leash on tops
•PARKING•	Several car parks throughout Llanberis
•PUBLIC TOILETS•	Just off High Street, south of tourist information centre

BACKGROUND TO THE WALK

Llanberis is a slate town, you can see that by looking across Llyn Padarn to the dismal purple-grey terraces that have been built into the mountainside. However it's easy to look the other way, to where Snowdon reigns supreme in the skies.

In Victorian times the interest in mountains was in its infancy. Being Wales' highest peak, attention was centred on Snowdon and the village at its foot. The Snowdon Mountain Railway was built, and opened on Easter Monday 1896 with a fanfare of publicity. Unfortunately, on that first day, a descending train ran out of control and was derailed round a bend, before tumbling down steep slopes. One passenger who jumped from a falling carriage was killed. Since then the steam engines on the rack-and-pinion railway have chugged up the mountain pushing their red and cream carriages for 4½ miles (7.2km) to the summit without incident. Though a few resent the trains' presence, most walkers are comforted by the whistles that pierce the mountain mists or the plumes of white smoke billowing into a clear blue sky.

The route through the Arddu Valley is a pleasing and peaceful way into the hills. In the early stages you'll ease by the shaly flanks of Moel Eilio before climbing to a dark pass on the Eilio–Snowdon ridge. The mile-long (1.6km) route from the pass to Moel Cynghorion is a bit of a grind, but the summit reveals your prize – a headlong view of Clogwyn Du'r Arddu's black cliffs and several remote tarns basking in two cwms below.

The route joins the Snowdon Ranger Path and zig-zags up Cloggy's rocky arm to Bwlch Glas, where you meet the crowds. Here, you gaze into Cwm Dyli, where the blue-green lakes of Glaslyn and Llydaw lie beneath the ridges of Carnedd Ugain, Crib Goch, and Y Lliwedd.

Now those crowds will lead you alongside the railway to gain the pile of rocks capping Snowdon's highest summit, Yr Wyddfa, or to one of the world's most unprepossessing hostelries, where you can buy refreshments. Snowdon's summit panorama is stunning and I will not try to list all the peaks in view: be content to know that you can see half of Wales laid out at your feet. Look further to the distant misty mountains in Ireland and the Isle of Man stretching across the horizon. Our way down Snowdon is easier than the way up: you could even catch the train had you a mind to. The Llanberis Path is long but it descends in gentle gradients across bare hillsides above the rugged fields of the Arddu Valley.

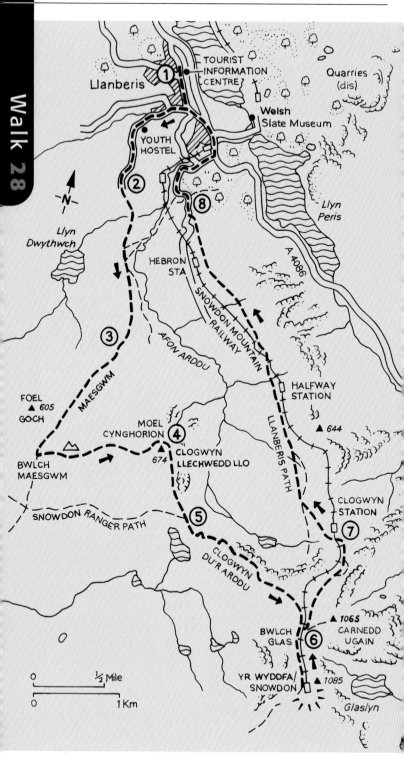

Walk 28 Directions

① From the tourist information centre in the heart of Llanberis, head south along the **High Street** (Stryd Fawr) before turning right up **Capel Coch Road**. Go straight ahead at a junction, where the road changes its name to **Stryd Ceunant**, and follow the road past the youth hostel. The road winds and climbs towards Brych y Foel, the north east spur of Moel Eilio.

② Where the tarmac ends at the foot of **Moel Eilio**, continue along the track, which swings left (south east) into the wild cwm of the Afon Arddu. On the other side of the cwm you'll see the trains of the Snowdon Mountain Railway, puffing up and down the line.

③ On reaching the base of Foel Goch's northern spur, **Cefn Drum**, the track swings right into **Maesgwm** and climbs to a pass, **Bwlch Maesgwm**, between Foel Goch and **Moel Cynghorion**. Go through the gate here, then turn left for the steep climb by the fence and up the latter-mentioned peak.

④ From Cynghorion's summit the route descends along the top of the cliffs of **Clogwyn Llechwedd Llo** to another pass, **Bwlch Cwm Brwynog**, which overlooks the small reservoir of Llyn Ffynnon-y-gwas. Here you join the **Snowdon Ranger Path**.

> **WHAT TO LOOK FOR** ⓘ
> **Yr Wyddfa** means the grave. The pile of stones on the summit is supposedly the grave of giant Rhita Gawr, who attempted to rob King Arthur of his beard. Arthur decapitated Rhita with his sword and the giant's head was left where it fell.

⑤ Follow the zig-zag route up **Clogwyn Du'r Arddu**, whose cliffs, on the left, plummet to a little tarn, Llyn Du'r Arddu, which sits uneasily in a dark stony cwm. Near the top the wide path veers right, away from the edge, meets the **Snowdon Mountain Railway**, and follows the line to the monolith at **Bwlch Glas**. Here you are met by both the Llanberis Path and the Pyg Track and look down on the huge cwms of Glaslyn and Llyn Llydaw.

> **WHILE YOU'RE THERE** ⓘ
> The **Welsh Slate Museum** by the lake gives an insight into the story of slate. The tour is introduced by a 3D show and there are demonstrations by craftspeople.

⑥ The path now follows the line of the railway to the summit. Retrace your steps to Bwlch Glas, but this time follow the wide **Llanberis Path** traversing the western slopes of Carnedd Ugain and above the railway. (Make sure you don't mistake this for the higher ridge path to Carnedd Ugain's summit.)

> **WHERE TO EAT AND DRINK** ⓘ
> **Pete's Eats** on the High Street in Llanberis is one of the best chippys in the world and, if you're in a mood to be self-indulgent, look no further.

⑦ Near **Clogwyn Station** you come to Cwm Hetiau, where cliffs fall away into the chasm of the Pass of Llanberis. The path goes under the railway here and passes below Clogwyn Station before recrossing the line near **Halfway Station**.

⑧ The path meets a lane beyond **Hebron**, and this descends back into Llanberis near the **Royal Victoria Hotel**. Turn left along the main road, then take the left fork, **High Street**, to get back to the car.

Walk 29

A Walk to White Nancy Above Bollington

Exploring a short but scenic ridge, with a strange landmark, above the leafy town of Bollington.

•DISTANCE•	3½ miles (5.7km)
•MINIMUM TIME•	2hrs
•ASCENT / GRADIENT•	1,180ft (360m) ▲ ▲ ▲
•LEVEL OF DIFFICULTY•	犮犮 犮犮 犮
•PATHS•	Easy field paths and farm tracks, one short, sharp descent
•LANDSCAPE•	Mostly gentle rolling pasture and small pockets of woodland
•SUGGESTED MAP•	aqua3 OS Explorer OL24 White Peak
•START / FINISH•	Grid reference: SJ 937775
•DOG FRIENDLINESS•	On lead through farmland, but off lead along lanes
•PARKING•	Kerbside parking on Church Street or Lord Street, Bollington
•PUBLIC TOILETS•	Bollington town centre

BACKGROUND TO THE WALK

Bollington lies just outside the far western edge of the Peak District National Park, but it continues to attract walkers and sightseers due in part to the short but inviting ridge of Kerridge Hill that overlooks the small Cheshire town. However it's not just the superb views that will hold your attention, but also the curiously shaped monument that occupies the far northern tip of the hill.

Striking Monument

Visible from below, and for some distance around for that matter since it stands at 920ft (280m) above sea level, White Nancy is a round stone construction that was built by the local Gaskell family in 1820 to commemorate the Battle of Waterloo. It was originally an open shelter with a stone table and benches, and was presumably a popular spot for picnics, but gradual decay and occasional vandalism led to it being bricked up, and now the building has no discernible door or windows. Nor does it bear any plaque or information panel, and most striking of all it is painted bright white. In terms of shape it resembles a large bell, or perhaps a giant chess pawn, with a large base that tapers into an odd little point. As for its name the most entertaining version suggests that Nancy was the name of one of the eight horses that pulled the heavy stone table to the summit when the tower was built. Beacons are still lit next to it to mark special occasions.

Stone Quarries

For all its scenic qualities the lower western slopes of Kerridge Hill are still quarried, although it's not visible on the walk until you reach the main summit ridge. The dressed stone is used for roofing slates and paving slabs and originally it was removed via narrow boats on the Macclesfield Canal that also served the mills and factories that once dotted the Bollington area. For a while shallow pits in the hill even yielded enough coal to supply the local engine houses, as steam power replaced water power during the Industrial Revolution's relentless advance. But inevitably your eye will be drawn to sights further afield, and if the weather is clear there will be good views across Macclesfield and the Cheshire Plain to the Mersey Estuary, the urban sprawl of Greater Manchester, as well as the long, high outline of the Pennines away to the north. Meanwhile White Nancy continues to sit impassively, a fittingly ambiguous monument to a past era when people felt compelled to mark the winning of a great overseas battle by building a picnic shelter on top of a small hill in Cheshire.

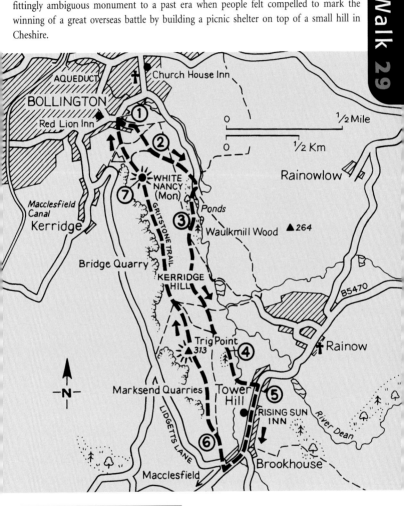

Walk 29 **Directions**

① The walk starts towards the top of **Lord Street** (which Church Street leads into) where it turns sharply right at the top of a steep hill. Go along **Cow Lane**, a cul-de-sac, and through the gate at the far end. Take the upper of two field

paths, quickly passing into a larger sloping field on the right. Aim for the gate and cattle grid at the far left top corner.

② Turn left on to an open farm track and follow this all the way down to the lane in the bottom of the valley. Turn right, and then almost immediately fork right again

Walk 29

WHILE YOU'RE THERE ⓘ

The **Highwayman**, a historic 16th-century inn on the B5470 north east of nearby Rainow, is reputed to be one of the most haunted in the Peak District. It's known locally as 'the Patch', and the small dark rooms, with their low beams, log fires and ornate wooden furniture exude character. But keep an eye out for the smoke rings that appear mysteriously in the middle room, and the old man in the snug bar that no one seems to know!

past some terraced cottages. A weir and pond below on your left are all that remain of the former silk mill. Follow this path through the Woodland Trust's **Waulkmill Wood**.

③ Leave the wood via a stile and go across the lower part of a sloping field, then in the second aim for the buildings on the far side. Follow the gated path around to the right, and on through successive fields.

④ Go over a stile with a Gritstone Trail waymark (a footprint with the letter 'G') and along the bottom edge of a very new, mixed plantation, then down a walled track through woodland to reach the main road at **Tower Hill**.

⑤ Turn right and walk along the pavement, past the **Rising Sun Inn**, for ½ mile (800m). Turn right into **Lidgetts Lane**, then as it bends almost immediately right go over a high stile ahead and on to a gated track past a row of hawthorn trees.

Swinging left follow this grassy path up to the ridge above – ignore the lower route by the right-hand fence.

⑥ Follow the obvious hilltop track all the way along the spine of **Kerridge Hill**, ignoring tracks off left and right.

⑦ After admiring the views at the monument (**White Nancy**) at the far end, drop sharply down the eroded path beyond, with Bollington spread out below, then cross a sunken farm lane and continue down across two more steep fields to reach a stile back into **Cow Lane/Lord Street**.

WHERE TO EAT AND DRINK ⓘ

Bollington has a staggering number of pubs and community clubs (over 20 at the last count!), as well as a few cafés and a cheerful bakery on the main road (B5090). But in terms of access to the walk try the **Church House Inn** at the bottom of Church Street and the **Red Lion Inn** at the top of Lord Street; and at Tower Hill (half way along the walk) the **Rising Sun Inn**. All serve food and drink at lunchtime and evenings.

WHAT TO LOOK FOR ⓘ

In the mid-1800s there were as many as 13 mills in Bollington, spinning cotton and silk, and later synthetic fibres such as rayon. The last cotton mill closed in 1960, but as you may see towards the bottom of Lord Street and elsewhere some of the town's surviving **mill buildings** have a new lease of life as modern offices and flats. Another fascinating throwback to a previous industrial age is the impressive Telford-designed **aqueduct**, which carries the Macclesfield Canal high above the main road through Bollington.

Cromford and the Black Rocks

Walk through the Industrial Revolution in a valley where history was made.

•**DISTANCE**•	5 miles (8km)
•**MINIMUM TIME**•	3hrs
•**ASCENT / GRADIENT**•	720ft (220m) ▲▲▲
•**LEVEL OF DIFFICULTY**•	🚶 🚶🚶 🚶🚶
•**PATHS**•	Well-graded – canal tow paths, lanes, forest paths and a railway trackbed, quite a few stiles
•**LANDSCAPE**•	Town streets and wooded hillsides
•**SUGGESTED MAP**•	aqua3 OS Explorer OL24 White Peak
•**START / FINISH**•	Grid reference: SK 300571
•**DOG FRIENDLINESS**•	Dogs on leads over farmland, can run free on long stretches of enclosed railway trackbed
•**PARKING**•	Cromford Wharf pay car park
•**PUBLIC TOILETS**•	At car park

BACKGROUND TO THE WALK

For many centuries Cromford, 'the ford by the bend in the river', was no more than a sleepy backwater. Lead mining brought the village brief prosperity, but by the 18th century even that was in decline. Everything changed in 1771 when Sir Richard Arkwright decided to build the world's first watered-powered cotton-spinning mill here. Within 20 years he had built two more, and had constructed a whole new town around them. Cromford was awake to the Industrial Revolution and would be connected to the rest of Britain by a network of roads, railways and canals.

As you walk through the cobbled courtyard of the Arkwright Mill, now being restored by the Arkwright Society, you are transported back into that austere world of the 18th century, back to the times when mother, father and children all worked at the mills.

Most of the town lies on the other side of the busy A6, including the mill pond which was built by Arkwright to impound the waters of Bonsall Brook, and the beautifully restored mill workers' cottages of North Street.

The Black Rocks

The Black Rocks overlook the town from the south. The walk makes a beeline for them through little ginnels, past some almshouses and through pine woods. You'll see climbers grappling with the 80ft (24m) gritstone crags, but there's a good path all the way to the top. Here you can look across the Derwent Valley to the gaunt skeleton of Riber Castle, to the beacon on top of Crich Stand and down the Derwent Gorge to Matlock.

The Cromford and High Peak Railway

The next stage of the journey takes you on to the High Peak Trail, which uses the former trackbed of the Cromford and High Peak Railway. Engineered by Josias Jessop, and built in the 1830s the railway was built as an extension of the canal system and, as such, the stations were called wharfs. In the early years horses pulled the wagons on the level stretches, while steam-winding engines worked the inclines. By the mid-1800s steam engines worked the whole line, which connected with the newly-extended Midland Railway. The railway was closed by Dr Beeching in 1967.

The Canal

After abandoning the High Peak Trail pleasant forest paths lead you down into the valley at High Peak Junction, where the old railway met the Cromford Canal. The 33-mile (53.5km) canal was built in 1793, a year after Arkwright's death, to link up with the Erewash, thus completing a navigable waterway to the River Trent at Trent Lock. Today, there's an information centre here, a fascinating place to muse before that final sojourn along the tow path to Cromford.

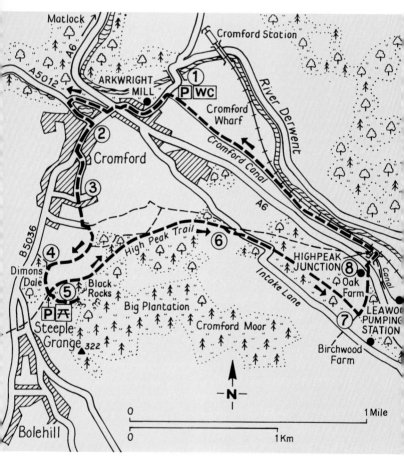

Walk 30 **Directions**

① Turn left out of the car park on to **Mill Road**. Cross the A6 to the **Market Place**. Turn right down the **Scarthin**, passing the **Boat Inn** and the old millpond before doubling back left along **Water Lane** to **Cromford Hill**.

② Turn right, past the shops and **Bell Inn**, then turn left up **Bedehouse Lane**, which turns into a narrow tarmac ginnel after rounding some almshouses (otherwise known as bedehouses).

③ At the top of the lane by a street of 1970s housing, a signpost for **Black Rocks** points uphill. The footpath continues its climb southwards to meet a lane. Turn left along the winding lane, which soon divides. Take the right fork, a limestone track leading to a stone-built house with woods behind. On reaching the house, turn right through a gate, and follow the top field edge.

④ After climbing some steps, ascend left through the woods of **Dimons Dale** up to the **Black Rocks** car park and picnic site. The track you've reached is on the former trackbed of the **Cromford and High Peak Railway**. Immediately opposite is the there-and-back waymarked detour leading to the rocks.

⑤ Returning to the car park, turn right along the **High Peak Trail**, which traverses the hillside high above **Cromford**.

⑥ After about ¾ mile (1.2km) watch out for a path on the right leaving the Trail for **Intake Lane**. On reaching the lane, turn right and follow it to a sharp left-hand bend. Here, go straight on,

following a path heading south east along the top edge of some woodland. (**Note:** Neither the path nor the wood is shown on the current Ordnance Survey Explorer OL map of the White Peak.)

⑦ On nearing **Birchwood Farm**, watch out for two paths coming up from the left. Take the one descending more directly downhill (north west, then north). At the bottom of the woods the path swings left across fields, coming out to the A6 road by **Oak Farm**.

⑧ Cross the road and follow the little ginnel opposite, over the **Matlock railway** and the **Cromford Canal**. Go past the **High Peak Junction** information centre, then turn left along the canal tow path. Follow this back to the car park at **Cromford Wharf**.

Walk 31

Lead Mining and the Transparent Stream

Lathkill Dale contrasts the wastes of a long-past lead-mining industry with the purity of its water.

•DISTANCE•	5 miles (8km)
•MINIMUM TIME•	3hrs
•ASCENT / GRADIENT•	984ft (300m) ▲▲▲
•LEVEL OF DIFFICULTY•	🚶🚶🚶
•PATHS•	Generally well-defined paths. Limestone dale sides can be slippery after rain, lots of stiles
•LANDSCAPE•	Partially wooded limestone dales
•SUGGESTED MAP•	aqua3 OS Explorer OL24 White Peak
•START / FINISH•	Grid reference: SK 203657
•DOG FRIENDLINESS•	Dogs on leads
•PARKING•	Over Haddon pay car park
•PUBLIC TOILETS•	At car park

BACKGROUND TO THE WALK

> *Lathkin is, by many degrees, the purest, the most transparent stream that I ever yet saw either at home or abroad…*
>
> Charles Cotton, 1676

Today, when you descend the winding lane into this beautiful limestone dale, you're confronted by ash trees growing beneath tiered limestone crags, tumbling screes, multi pastel-coloured grasslands swaying in the breeze and that same crystal stream, still full of darting trout.

Invasion of the Lead Miners

Yet it was not always so. In the 18th and 19th century lead miners came here and stripped the valley of its trees. They drilled shafts and adits into the white rock, built pump houses, elaborate aqueducts, waterwheels and tramways; and when the old schemes failed to realise the intended profits they came up with new, even bigger ones. Inevitably nobody made any real money, and by 1870 the price of lead had slumped from overseas competition and the pistons finally stopped.

On this walk you will see the fading but still fascinating remnants of this past, juxtaposed with a seemingly natural world that is gradually reclaiming the land. In reality it's English Nature, who are managing the grasslands and woods as part of the Derbyshire Dales National Nature Reserve. The walk starts with a narrow winding lane from Over Haddon to a clapper bridge by Lathkill Lodge. A lush tangle of semi-aquatic plants surround the river and the valley sides are thick with ash and sycamore. In spring you're likely to see nesting moorhens and mallards. In the midst of the trees are some mossy pillars, the remains of an aqueduct built to supply a head of water for the nearby Mandale Mine. The path leaves the woods and the character of the dale changes markedly once again. Here sparse ash trees grow out of the limestone screes, where herb Robert adds splashes of pink.

Disappearing River

In the dry periods of summer the river may have disappeared completely beneath its permeable bed of limestone. The sun-dried soils on the southern slopes are too thin to support the humus loving plants of the valley bottom. Instead, here you'll see the pretty early purple orchid, cowslips with their yellowy primrose-like flowers and clumps of the yellow-flowered rock rose.

After climbing out of Cales Dale the walk traverses the high fields of the White Peak plateau. If you haven't already seen them, look out for Jacob's ladder, a 3ft (1m) tall, increasingly rare plant with clusters of bell-like purple-blue flowers.By the time you have crossed the little clapper bridge by Lathkill Lodge and climbed back up that winding lane to the car park, you will have experienced one of Derbyshire's finest dales.

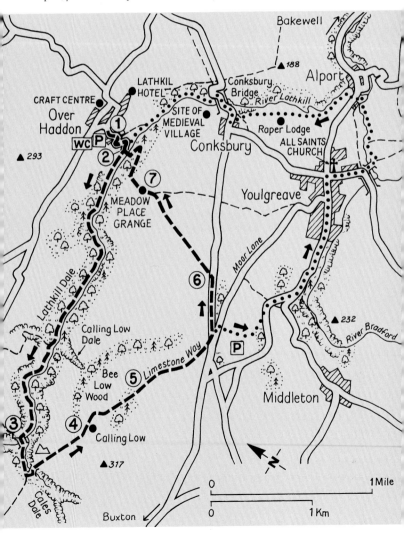

Walk 31 Directions

Walk 31

① Turn right out of the car park, and descend the narrow tarmac lane, which winds down into **Lathkill Dale**.

② Just before reaching **Lathkill Lodge** and the river, turn right along a concessionary track that runs parallel to the north bank. The path passes several caves and a mineshaft as it weaves its way through woodland and thick vegetation. South of **Haddon Grove** the trees thin out to reveal the fine limestone crags and screes of the upper dale. The path now is rougher as it traverses an area of screes.

③ Go over the footbridge and follow a little path sneaking into **Cales Dale**. Take the left fork down to a footbridge across the stream, which could well be dry outside the winter months. You now join the **Limestone Way** long distance route on a stepped path climbing eastwards out of the dale and on to the high pastures of **Calling Low**.

④ The path heads east of south east across the fields then, just before **Calling Low** farm, diverts left (waymarked) through several small

wooded enclosures. The path swings right beyond the farm, then half left across a cow-pocked field to its top left-hand corner and some woods.

⑤ Over steps in the wall the path cuts a corner through the woods before continuing through more fields to reach a tarmac lane, where you turn left.

⑥ After about 500yds (457m), follow a signposted footpath that begins at a stile in a dry-stone wall on the left. This heads north east across fields to the huge farming complex of **Meadow Place Grange**. Waymarks show you the way across the cobbled courtyard, where the path continues between two stable blocks into another field.

⑦ After heading north across the field to the brow of **Lathkill Dale**, turn right through a gate on to a zig-zag track descending to the river. Cross the old clapper bridge to **Lathkill Lodge** and follow the outward route, a tarmac lane, back to the car park.

Extending the Walk

You can see the lower part of **Lathkill Dale** by leaving the main route as shown and descending through **Youlgreave** village to **Alport** from where a riverside path will take you all the way back to the start of the walk, at the bottom of the hill near **Over Haddon**.

On the Moorland's Edge

To Lantern Pike and Middle Moor above the Sett Valley above Hayfield.

•DISTANCE•	7 miles (11.3km)
•MINIMUM TIME•	4hrs
•ASCENT / GRADIENT•	1,640ft (500m) ▲▲▲
•LEVEL OF DIFFICULTY•	🧍🧍 🧍🧍 🧍🧍
•PATHS•	Good paths and tracks, plenty of stiles
•LANDSCAPE•	Heather moorland, and rolling farm pastures
•SUGGESTED MAP•	aqua3 OS Explorer OL1 Dark Peak
•START / FINISH•	Grid reference: SK 036869
•DOG FRIENDLINESS•	Walk is on farmland and access agreement land. Dogs should be kept on leads
•PARKING•	Sett Valley Trail pay car park, Hayfield
•PUBLIC TOILETS•	At car park

BACKGROUND TO THE WALK

Hayfield was busy. It had cotton mills, it had papermaking mills and it had calico printing and dye factories. Hayfield had times of trouble. Floods washed away three bridges, even swept away some bodies from their churchyard graves. And in 1830 it resounded to marching feet, not the feet of ramblers, but those of a thousand protesting mill workers, demanding a living wage. As was always the case in such times, the men were beaten back by soldiers and charged with civil disorder. Their industry went into a slow decline that would last a century, and Hayfield returned to its countryside ways.

The Sett Valley Trail
The first part of the walk to little Lantern Pike follows the Sett Valley Trail, the trackbed of a railway that until 1970 linked Manchester and New Mills with Hayfield. At its peak the steam train would have brought thousands of people from Manchester. Today it's a pleasant tree-lined track, working its way through the valley between the hills of Lantern Pike and Chinley Churn. The track, and its former wasteland surroundings, are becoming quite a haven for wildlife. Beneath the ash, sycamore, beech and oak you'll see wood anemone, bluebells and wild garlic along with the rhubarb-like butterbur. In the days before fridges butterbur leaves were used to wrap butter to keep it cool.

Lantern Pike
Lantern Pike is the middle of three ridges peeping through the trees, and by the time you get to Birch Vale you're ready to tackle it. So up you go, on a shady path through woods, then a country lane with wild flowers in the verges, and finally on heather and grass slopes to the rocky-crested summit. Lantern Pike's name comes from the beacon tower that once stood on its summit. Fortunately for countrygoers, it had to be demolished in 1907 after falling into a dangerous state of disrepair. Having descended back down to the busy Glossop road the route then climbs up across Middle Moor where it enters a new landscape – one of expansive heather fields. Soon you're on the skyline looking down on the Kinder and the

ever-so-green valley beneath your feet. This seems to be complemented to perfection by the shapely and ever-so-green peaks of Mount Famine and South Head.

Into Modern Hayfield

You come down to Hayfield on the Snake Path, an old traders' route linking the Sett and Woodland valleys. A fine street of stone-built cottages, with window boxes overflowing with flowers, takes you to the centre. This is a place where walkers come, and motorists take tea before motoring somewhere else. It's all so very peaceful – now.

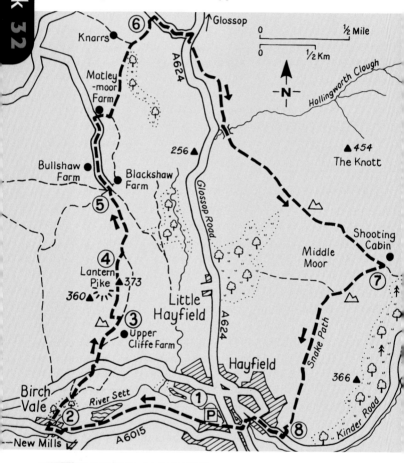

Walk 32 Directions

① Follow the old railway trackbed signposted 'The Sett Valley Trail', from the western end of the car park in Hayfield. This heads west down the valley and above the River Sett to meet the A6015 New Mills road at **Birch Vale**.

② Turn right along the road, then right again along a cobbled track behind the cottages of the **Crescent** into the shade of woods. Beyond a gate, the track meets a tarred farm lane at a hairpin bend. Follow the higher course to reach a country lane. Staggered to the right across it, a tarred bridleway climbs further up the hillside. Take the left fork near

Upper Cliffe Farm to a gate at the edge of the **National Trust's Lantern Pike** site.

③ Leave the bridleway here and turn left along a grassy wallside path climbing heather and bracken slopes to the rock-fringed ridge. Turn right and climb the airy crest to **Lantern Pike**'s summit, which is topped by a view indicator.

> **WHERE TO EAT AND DRINK** ℹ
> **Twenty Trees Café** in Hayfield serves good food, including filled jacket potatoes, bacon sandwiches, cakes and salads. Drinks and bar meals can be had at the **Royal Hotel** in Hayfield.

④ The path continues northwards from the top of Lantern Pike, descending to a gate at the northern boundary of the National Trust estate, where it rejoins the track you left earlier. Follow this now across high pastures to a five-way footpath signpost to the west of Blackshaw Farm.

⑤ Turn left along the walled farm lane past **Bullshaw Farm**, then right on a track passing the buildings of **Matleymoor Farm**. Where the track swings to the right leave it for a rough grassy track on the left. Go over the stile at its end and continue northwards on a grooved path, which joins a surfaced track from **Knarrs**.

⑥ Turn right along the track to reach the A624 road. Cross this with care and go over the stile at the far side. Turn immediately right, following a faint, rutted track with a wall on the right-hand side. This crosses the little valley of **Hollingworth Clough** on a footbridge before climbing up the heather slopes of **Middle Moor**.

> **WHAT TO LOOK FOR** ℹ
> **Lantern Pike** was donated to the National Trust in 1950, after being purchased by subscription. It was to be a memorial to Edwin Royce, who fought for the freedom to roam these hills. A summit view indicator, commemorating Royce's life and struggle, records the 360 degree panorama.

⑦ By a white shooting cabin you turn right on the stony **Snake Path**, which descends through heather at first, then, beyond a kissing gate, across fields to reach a stony walled track. Follow it down to **Kinder Road** near the centre of **Hayfield**.

> **WHILE YOU'RE THERE** ℹ
> Take a look round **Hayfield**. It has many old houses, former mills and cottages. The Pack Horse Inn on Kinder Road, for instance, dates back to 1577. The Royal Hotel was visited by John Wesley in 1755 – but in those days it was still the local parsonage.

⑧ Turn right down the lane, then left down steps to **Church Street**. Turn left to **St Matthew's Church**, then right down a side street signed to the **Sett Valley Trail**. This leads to the busy main road. Cross with care back to the car park.

Ghosts of Miller's Dale

The rural serenity of modern Miller's Dale belies its early role in the Industrial Revolution.

•**DISTANCE**•	6 miles (9.7km)
•**MINIMUM TIME**•	4hrs
•**ASCENT / GRADIENT**•	690ft (210m) ▲▲▲
•**LEVEL OF DIFFICULTY**•	🚶🚶 🚶
•**PATHS**•	Generally well-defined paths and tracks, path in Water-cum-Jolly Dale liable to flooding, quite a few stiles
•**LANDSCAPE**•	Limestone dales
•**SUGGESTED MAP**•	aqua3 OS Explorer OL24 White Peak
•**START / FINISH**•	Grid reference: SK 154743
•**DOG FRIENDLINESS**•	Dogs could run free in dales with no livestock, but kept under control when crossing farmland
•**PARKING**•	Tideswell Dale pay car park
•**PUBLIC TOILETS**•	At car park

BACKGROUND TO THE WALK

It's all quiet in Miller's Dale these days, but it wasn't always so. Many early industrialists wanted to build their cotton mills in the countryside, far away from the marauding Luddites of the city. The Wye and its tributaries had the power to work these mills. The railway followed, and that brought more industry with it. And so little Miller's Dale and its neighbours joined the Industrial Revolution.

The walk starts in Tideswell Dale. Nowadays it's choked with thickets and herbs but they hide a history of quarrying and mining. Here the miners wanted basalt, a dark, hard igneous rock that was used for road building.

Cruelty at the Mill

Litton Mill will eventually be modernised into holiday cottages, but today it lies damp and derelict in a shadowy part of the dale. *The Memoirs of Robert Blincoe*, written in 1863, tells of mill owner Ellis Needham's cruelty to child apprentices, who were often shipped in from the poorhouses of London. Many of the children died and were buried in the churchyards of Tideswell and Taddington. It is said that ghosts of some of the apprentices still make appearances in or around the mill. The walk emerges from the shadows of the mill into Water-cum-Jolly Dale. At first the river is lined by mudbanks thick with rushes and common horsetail. It's popular with wildfowl. The river widens out and, at the same time, impressive limestone cliffs squeeze the path. The river's widening is artificial, a result of it being controlled to form a head of water for the downstream mill.

Round the next corner is Cressbrook Mill, built by Sir Richard Arkwright, but taken over by William Newton. Newton also employed child labour but was said to have treated them well. The rooftop bell tower would have peeled to beckon the apprentices, who lived next door, to the works. Like Litton this impressive Georgian mill was allowed to moulder, but is now being restored as flats. The walk leaves the banks of the Wye at Cressbrook to take in pretty Cressbrook Dale. In this nature reserve you'll see lily-of-the-valley, wild garlic and bloody cranesbill; you should also see bee and fragrant orchids. Just as you think you've found your true rural retreat you'll climb to the rim of the dale, look across it and see the grassed-over spoil heaps of lead mines. Finally, the ancient strip fields of Litton form a mosaic of pasture and dry-stone wall on the return to Tideswell Dale.

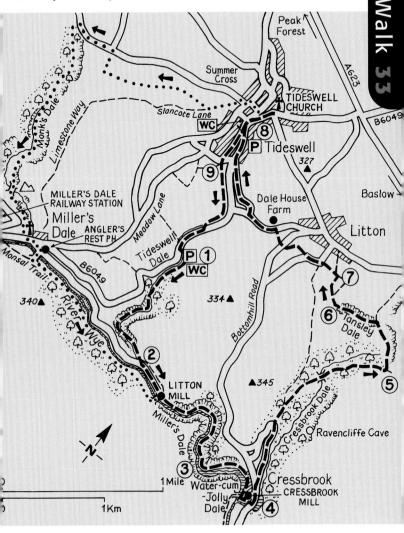

Walk 33 Directions

① Follow the path southwards from beside the car park's toilet block into **Tideswell Dale**, taking the right-hand fork to cross over the little bridge.

② On entering **Miller's Dale**, go left along the tarmac lane to **Litton Mill**. Go through the gateposts on to a concessionary path through the mill yard. Beyond the mill, the path follows the **River Wye**, as it meanders through the tight, steep-sided dale.

Walk 33

③ The river widens out in **Water-cum-Jolly Dale** and the path, liable to flooding here, traces a wall of limestone cliffs before reaching **Cressbrook**. Do not cross the bridge on the right, but turn left to pass in front of **Cressbrook Mill** and out on to the road.

④ Turn left along the road, then take the right fork which climbs steadily into **Cressbrook Dale**. Where the road doubles back uphill leave it for a track going straight ahead into the woods. The track degenerates into a narrow path that emerges in a clearing high above the stream. Follow it downhill to a footbridge over the stream, then take the right fork path, which climbs high up the valley side to a stile in the top wall.

WHILE YOU'RE THERE ℹ
Millers Dale Railway Station is a fascinating old site with a good deal of information on the railway, the wildlife and the walking. The station was built in 1863 for the Midland Railway. The line closed in 1967 and wild flowers now line the sides of the trackbed.

---

⑤ Do not cross the stile, but take the downhill path to the dale bottom, where there's a junction of paths. The one wanted here recrosses the stream on stepping stones, and climbs into **Tansley Dale**.

⑥ The path turns right at the top of the dale, follows a tumbledown wall before crossing it on a step stile. Head for a wall corner in the next field, then veer right through a narrow enclosure to reach a walled track just south of **Litton village**.

⑦ Turn left along the track, which comes out on to a country lane at the crown of a sharp bend. Keep

---

WHAT TO LOOK FOR ℹ
Cressbrook Dale is part of the Derbyshire Dales National Nature Reserve. On the limestone grassland you may see orchids, cranesbill, mountain pansy, globeflower and spring sandwort. One of the many limestone-loving plants is the Nottingham catchfly, which loves dry, stony places. The white flowers roll back in daytime, but are fragrant at night. Small insects are often caught on the sticky stalks but nature is being wasteful, for they're never devoured by the plant.

---

straight on down the lane but leave it at the next bend for a cross-field path to **Bottomhill Road**. Across the road, a further field path descends to the lane at **Dale House Farm**. Turn left, then right on a lane marked unsuitable for motors. Follow this road into **Tideswell**.

⑧ After looking around the village head south down the main street, then right on to **Gordon Road**, which then heads south.

⑨ Where this ends, continue down the stony track ahead, which runs parallel with the main road. Watch for a stile on the left, which gives access to a path, down to the road into **Tideswell Dale**. Turn right along the road, back to the car park.

Extending the Walk
If it's dry you can extend this walk though **Monk's Dale**. Leave the main route at Point ⑧ in **Tideswell** and rejoin it from the **Monsal Trail**, back at **Litton Mill**, near Point ②, to retrace your steps to the start.

WHERE TO EAT AND DRINK ℹ
The atmospheric **Anglers Rest** pub at Miller's Dale and the **Hills and Dales Tearooms** in Tideswell are both recommended for their warm welcome to weary walkers.

Bradfield and the Dale Dike Dam Disaster

A quiet waterside walk around the site of a horrific 19th-century industrial tragedy.

•DISTANCE•	5½ miles (8.8km)
•MINIMUM TIME•	3hrs 30min
•ASCENT / GRADIENT•	394ft (120m) ▲ ▲ ▲
•LEVEL OF DIFFICULTY•	🚶 🚶 🚶
•PATHS•	Minor roads, bridleways, forest paths
•LANDSCAPE•	Woodland, reservoir and meadows
•SUGGESTED MAP•	aqua3 OS Explorer OL1 Dark Peak
•START / FINISH•	Grid reference: SK 262920
•DOG FRIENDLINESS•	Keep on lead near livestock
•PARKING•	By cricket ground in Bradfield
•PUBLIC TOILETS•	None on route

BACKGROUND TO THE WALK

Just before midnight on Friday 11 March 1864, when the Dale Dike Dam collapsed, 650 million gallons (2,955 million litres) of water surged along the Loxley Valley towards Sheffield, leaving a trail of death and destruction. When the floods finally subsided 244 people had been killed and hundreds of properties destroyed.

The Bradfield Scheme

During the Industrial Revolution Sheffield expanded rapidly, as country people sought employment in the city's steel and cutlery works. This put considerable pressure on the water supply. The 'Bradfield Scheme' was Sheffield Waterworks Company's ambitious proposal to build massive reservoirs in the hills around the village of Bradfield, about 8 miles (12.9km) from the city. Work commenced on the first of these, the Dale Dike Dam on 1 January 1859. It was a giant by the standards of the time with a capacity of over 700 million gallons (3,182 million litres) of water, but some 200 million gallons (910 million litres) less than the present reservoir.

The Disaster of 1864

Construction of the dam continued until late February 1864, by which time the reservoir was almost full. Friday 11 March was a stormy day and as one of the dam workers crossed the earthen embankment on his way home, he noticed a crack, about a finger's width, running along it. John Gunson the chief engineer turned out with one of the contractors to inspect the dam. They had to make the 8 miles (12.9km) from Sheffield in a horse-drawn gig, in deteriorating weather conditions, so it was 10PM before they got there. After an initial inspection, Gunson concluded that it was probably nothing to worry about. However as a precaution he decided to lower the water level. He re-inspected the crack at 11:30PM, noting that it had not visibly deteriorated. However, then the engineer saw to his horror that water was running over the top of the embankment into the crack. He was making his way to the bottom of the embankment when he felt the ground beneath him begin to shake and saw the top of the dam breached by the straining waters. He just had time to scramble up the side before a large section of the dam collapsed, unleashing a solid wall of water down into the valley below towards Sheffield. The torrent destroyed everything in its path and though the waters started to subside within half an hour their destructive force swept aside 415 houses, 106 factories or shops, 20 bridges and countless cottage and market gardens for 8 miles (12.9km). Men women and children were not spared, some whole families were wiped out, including an 87-year-old woman and a 2-day-old baby.

At the inquest the jury concluded that there had been insufficient engineering skill devoted to a work of such size and called for legislation to ensure 'frequent, sufficient and regular' inspections of dams. The Dale Dike Dam was rebuilt in 1875 but it was not brought into full use until 1887, a very dry year.

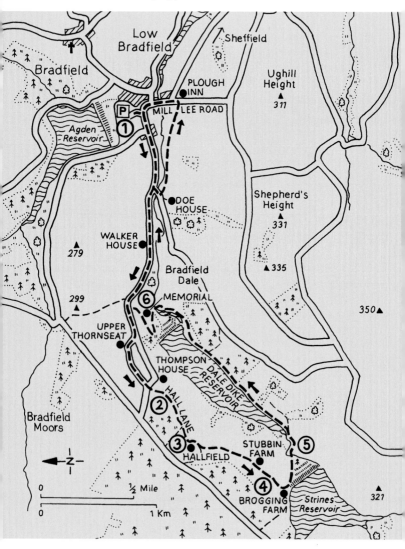

Walk 34 Directions

① Exit the car park and turn right on to the road. At a Y-junction go right towards Midhopestones. Follow this road uphill passing, on the right, a former inn, **Walker House** farm and **Upper Thornseat**. When the road turns sharply right, at the entrance to **Thomson House**, turn left on to the farm road.

② From here go through a gate in front of you and on to **Hall Lane**, a public bridleway. Follow this along the edge of a wood then through another gate and continue right on the farm road. Another gate at the end of this road leads to the entrance to **Hallfield**.

WHERE TO EAT AND DRINK ⓘ

The **Plough Inn** is over 200 years old and has held a licence for most of that time. A former farmhouse, it contains an enormous stone hearth, stone walls and traditional timbers. Real ales and traditional home-cooked food is the standard fare with a splendid selection of roasts on a Sunday. Children are very welcome if eating.

---

③ The right of way goes through the grounds of Hallfield but an alternative permissive path leads left over a stile, round the perimeter of the house and across another stile to re-join the bridleway at the back of the house. Follow the bridleway crossing a stile, a gate and then past **Stubbin Farm**.

④ The next gate leads to **Brogging Farm** and the dam at the head of Strines Reservoir. Look out for a sign near the end of the farmhouse and turn left. Go slightly downhill, over a stile, follow the path, then cross a stile and go through a wood.

⑤ Cross the stream by a footbridge, keep to the right, ignoring a second footbridge, then follow the path along the bank of **Dale Dike Reservoir** to the dam head. From here continue through the woods, down several sets of steps and continue on the path looking out for the memorial to those who were killed as a result of the dam breaching in 1864.

WHILE YOU'RE THERE ⓘ

Don't miss the Parish **Church of St Nicholas**, which dates from 1487. It contains a Norman font gifted by the Cistercian monks at Roche Abbey and a Saxon cross found at Low Bradfield in the late 19th century. But it is the Watch House at the gates of the church that sets it apart. Built in 1745 to prevent body snatching it is the last one to survive in Yorkshire.

---

⑥ Follow the path until it reaches the road. Cross the stile, turn right on to the road and proceed to the Y-Junction. Turn right, cross the bridge then look for a public footpath sign to Low Bradfield just before the entrance to **Doe House**. Cross the stile on the left and follow the path. The path crosses two stiles then terminates at a T-junction with **Mill Lee Road** opposite the **Plough Inn**. Turn left and follow this road downhill, through the village and back to the car park.

WHAT TO LOOK FOR ⓘ

A **memorial** was erected at the dam in 1991 to commemorate those who lost their lives in the flood. It's a simple memorial stone surrounded by a small garden. Next to it there's a white stone bearing the letters CLOB. This is one of four stones that mark the Centre Line of the Old Bank and are the only trace today of where the earthen embankment of the previous dam stood.

Walk 35

Rocks and Water at Anglezarke

A landscape shaped by quarries and reservoirs, full of interest both historical and natural.

•DISTANCE•	7 miles (11.3km)
•MINIMUM TIME•	2hrs 30min
•ASCENT / GRADIENT•	689ft (210m) ▲ ▲ ▲
•LEVEL OF DIFFICULTY•	🚶 🚶 🚶
•PATHS•	Mostly good tracks with some field paths, 20 stiles
•LANDSCAPE•	Woodland, reservoirs, open valleys and farmland
•SUGGESTED MAP•	aqua3 OS Explorer 287 West Pennine Moors
•START / FINISH•	Grid reference: SD 621161
•DOG FRIENDLINESS•	Can run free on reservoir tracks, sheep elsewhere
•PARKING•	Large car park at Anglezarke
•PUBLIC TOILETS•	Nearest at Rivington

BACKGROUND TO THE WALK

A string of reservoirs moats the western side of the high moors of Anglezarke and Rivington and quarries scar their flanks. This is not a pristine landscape by any stretch of the imagination, yet today it is seen by many as an oasis of tranquillity close to busy towns and a motorway.

Reclaimed by Nature

A gentle start just above the shores of Anglezarke Reservoir leads to Lester Mill Quarry, which was worked until the 1930s. The quarry wall is imposing, but somewhat vegetated, and the rock is loose in places. It is much less popular with climbers than Anglezarke Quarry. The name is one reminder that this valley was once a thriving agricultural community. The mill, which served the whole valley, was drowned by the reservoir in 1855. Cheap imports further weakened the rural economy. Today there is only one working farm east of the reservoir.

The route continues through a mix of woodland and pasture to the head of the lake, then heads up the valley below steep, bouldery Stronstrey Bank. There's another quarry high on the right near the end of the bank, seemingly guarded by a number of gaunt, dead trees. Just beyond is another, set further back. Just beyond this an impressive spillway testifies to the potential power of Dean Black Brook.

A Busy Industrial Village

Now you cross The Goit, a canal that feeds the reservoir, to White Coppice cricket ground. There's a small reservoir just above and you pass others on the way down to the present-day hamlet. These served the mills that flourished here for well over a century. Along with the quarries at Stronstrey Bank these made White Coppice a busy industrial village with a population which may have approached 200. The mill closed in 1914 and little remains today. The railway closed in the late 1950s, the school in 1963 and the church in 1984. This sounds like a story of decline yet today many people would see White Coppice as an idyllic place to live, a fact reflected in the local house prices.

View to Winter Hill

After White Coppice you climb to Healey Nab. Trees obscure what must have been a fine all-round view from the highest point, but there's a good southward prospect from the large cairn on Grey Heights. Winter Hill is the highest of the moors, unmistakable with its TV towers. The main mast is just over 1,000ft (305m) tall, so you could argue that its tip is the highest point in Lancashire. The string of reservoirs is also well displayed and you get a bird's eye view of Chorley.

The walk finishes across the Anglezarke dam and then, to minimise road walking, makes a short climb to the small Yarrow Reservoir. The final descent gives an opportunity to look into Anglezarke Quarry.

Walk 35 Directions

① Leave the car park by a kissing gate and follow a track near the water. Fork right, through **Lester Mill Quarry**, then go right, and straight on at the next junction. The track climbs a steep rise.

WHERE TO EAT AND DRINK ⓘ
The **Yew Tree**, at Lane Ends, 250yds (229m) from the Anglezarke dam, lacks cask beer but has a cosy atmosphere and a choice of bar food or a restaurant menu. Families are welcome and there's outside seating for those with dogs.

---

② Go through a gap on the left, on a bend. The path traverses a wooded slope. Descend steps, join a wider track and go left. Beyond a stile follow a narrower path until it meets a road.

③ Go left 50yds (46m) to a kissing gate. Follow a track up the valley below **Stronstrey Bank**. Cross a bridge then go through a kissing gate and over another bridge to **White Coppice cricket ground**.

④ Bear left up a lane, then follow tarmac into **White Coppice** hamlet. Cross a bridge by the post-box. Follow a stream then go up left by a reservoir. Bear left to a stile. Cross the next field to its top right corner and go right on a lane. Where it bends right go left up a track.

WHAT TO LOOK FOR ⓘ
Subtle differences in the nature of the **rock** can be seen in the different quarries. These were significant for the uses to which the stone could be put. Parts of Anglezarke Quarry are 'massive' – there are very few cracks. Some of the rock here is especially pure and was used to line blast furnaces.

---

⑤ Skirt **Higher Healey**, follow field edges, then angle up left into dark plantations. Fork left just inside, and ascend to an old quarry. Follow its rim for three-quarters of the way round then bear away left through a larch plantation.

⑥ Go left on a clear path then right to the large cairn on **Grey Heights**. Descend slightly right, winding down past a small plantation, and join a wider green track. Bear left over a small rise then follow a track to a lane by **White House farm**.

WHILE YOU'RE THERE ⓘ
On most days, but especially at weekends, there's a very good chance of seeing rock climbers in **Anglezarke Quarry**. It's one of the most popular venues in Lancashire. A recent guidebook listed 165 routes ranging in severity from Difficult (which isn't) to E6 (which is), and more have been added since.

---

⑦ Cross a stile on the left, below the farmyard wall, then bear left to the corner of the field. Cross the stile on the left then up the field edge and join a confined path. From a stile on the right follow trees along the field edge to a rough track. Go right and straight on to **Kays Farm**.

⑧ Go right down a track then left on a lane below the reservoir wall. As the lane angles away, go left over a stile then skirt the reservoir until pushed away from the water by a wood. Join the road across the dam. Go through a gap and up a steep track. Go left at the top round **Yarrow Reservoir** to a road.

⑨ Go left, passing the entrance to **Anglezarke Quarry**, to a junction. Go right, and the car park entrance is on the first bend.

Weaving Ways Around Wycoller and Trawden

A moderate walk around an upland district steeped in the history of Lancashire, Yorkshire and the textile industry.

•DISTANCE•	5¼ miles (8.4km)
•MINIMUM TIME•	2hrs
•ASCENT / GRADIENT•	538ft (165m) ▲ ▲ ▲
•LEVEL OF DIFFICULTY•	🚶 🚶 🚶
•PATHS•	Field paths, some rough tracks and quiet lanes, 19 stiles
•LANDSCAPE•	Upland pastures, moorland and wooded valley
•SUGGESTED MAP•	aqua3 OS Explorer OL21 South Pennines
•START / FINISH•	Grid reference: SD 926395
•DOG FRIENDLINESS•	Mostly on grazing land, dogs must be closely controlled
•PARKING•	Car park just above Wycoller village (no general access for vehicles to village itself)
•PUBLIC TOILETS•	In Wycoller village

BACKGROUND TO THE WALK

Everyone associates the Brontës with Yorkshire, but they had strong Lancashire connections too. As children the sisters lived in the north of the county, attending school at Cowan Bridge, only later moving to Haworth, where they wrote their famous books. Haworth is only 9 miles (14.5km) from Wycoller and today you can walk the distance on the Brontë Way.

Handloom Weavers

Another hint of Yorkshire is the tradition of weaving wool, rather than the cotton usually associated with Lancashire. Trawden had several mills. Wycoller was a community of handloom weavers but as the Industrial Revolution developed they were unable to compete with the growth of larger, powered mills and the village became an isolated backwater.

Sheep and Cattle

Naturally sheep farming is important here, especially on the higher ground, but the area has a long tradition of cattle rearing too. The distinctive walls of large upright slabs that are seen in places are known as vaccary walls – a vaccary being a cattle farm.

Quiet First Half

The first half of the walk crosses these pastures, though you'll see more sheep than cattle today. For much of the way you climb gently, with wide views towards Pendle and the Yorkshire Dales, finally emerging on to the open moors. The route now follows an old trackway along the edge of the moor before swinging back down into Turnhole Clough. The path skirts above the woods before dropping into them and crossing the beck. Just below you meet the main Wycoller Beck. About 300yds (274m) below the confluence is the Clam Bridge, believed to be more than 1,000 years old and made of a single massive slab of gritstone. At least, it was a single slab until 1989, when an exceptionally heavy flood swept the bridge away. It was repaired and replaced, but damaged again the following year. Though the repair has been skilfully done, you can clearly see where the slab was broken.

Wycoller Hamlet

Following the stream, you soon come into Wycoller hamlet. Despite its simple construction of stone slabs, the clapper bridge is a relatively recent affair, at most only 200 years old. The packhorse bridge is certainly more ancient, possibly over 700 years old. The low parapets, which sometimes alarm nervous parents (though usually not their children), are an essential feature for a packhorse bridge as the animals would be heavily burdened with huge bales of wool.

Broken Up

Near by stand the ruins of Wycoller Hall. Originally built in the 16th century, the Hall was considerably enlarged in the 18th century by Henry Cunliffe. Unfortunately the lavish works left him heavily in debt and after his death, in 1818, the estate was broken up. It's thought that the Hall was largely derelict by the time the Brontë sisters knew about it and that it inspired Ferndean Manor in Charlotte's *Jane Eyre* (1847).

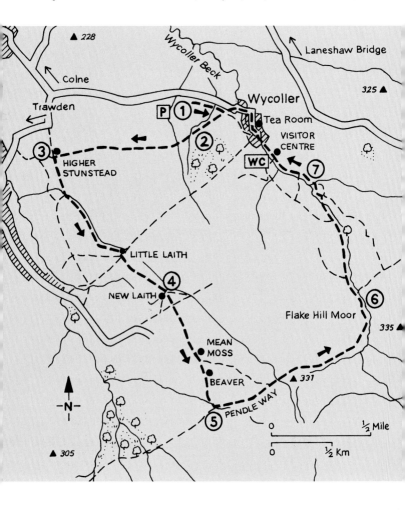

Walk 36 Directions

① At the top of the car park are a notice-board and a sign 'Wycoller 500m'. Follow the footpath indicated, just above the road, until it joins it on a bend. Cross a stile on the right and slant right across the field to another stile, then up to a gate and into a garden. Follow the arrow through trees up the left side to another stile.

WHILE YOU'RE THERE
Apart from a closer look at Wycoller itself, with its impressive new visitor centre, you could take a look at one of the more impressive sections of the **Leeds and Liverpool Canal** at Foulridge, just beyond Colne. Narrowboat cruises are available, some of which venture into the Foulridge Mile Tunnel.

② Bear right, cross a stream, then bear left, up towards a house on the skyline, until a footbridge and stile appear in a dip. Follow the hedge and then a wall in the same line. When it ends at open, rushy pasture bear slightly right (towards Pendle Hill, if clear). Cresting the rise, you'll see a stile and signpost by a corner of walls. The sign for Trawden points too far right. Aim slightly left, between two power line poles and again, once over a rise, you'll see a stile and signpost by the end of a fine wall. Follow the wall and then a walled track to **Higher Stunstead**. Go past the first buildings and into the yard.

WHERE TO EAT AND DRINK
There's a fine **tea room** in Wycoller itself, with a delightful garden. You can find pubs in Trawden and in Laneshaw Bridge on the A6068, where the **Emmot Arms** has a particularly good reputation for both food and beer.

③ Go left up a walled track to a cattle grid then ahead to a stile and follow the course of a stream up to **Little Laith**. Continue to pass the house on your left then go straight ahead, along field edges, to a large barn on the skyline by **New Laith**. Follow arrows round the farm.

④ Continue virtually straight ahead to a stile by a gate and over more stiles to **Mean Moss**. Go a few paces left up a track then follow the wall on the right and more stiles to **Beaver**. Go slightly right down a field to a stile near the corner then up by the stream to a track.

⑤ Go left, then keep straight on above the wall following a rougher continuation (Pendle Way sign). When the wall turns sharp left, the track bends more gradually, above a stream, down to another signpost.

WHAT TO LOOK FOR
Lively waters like those of Wycoller Beck are an ideal habitat for **dippers**. These small birds may often be seen perched on stones. The distinctive bobbing motion, which gives them their name, can make them hard to spot against the flickering background of running water. If you're lucky you may also see them 'flying underwater', as they feed largely on stream beds.

⑥ Go slightly left to a stile by a gate then take the lower path, down towards the stream then up round a wood. From a kissing gate drop down to cross the stream, then follow it down and out to a lane.

⑦ Go left down the lane to the **visitor centre** and **Wycoller** hamlet itself. From here, go left up the lane and join the outward part of the route for the last 350yds (320m) back to the car park.

Quenching the Thirst at Dovestones

A circular walk around the moorland reservoirs near Uppermill.

•DISTANCE•	7 miles (11.3km)
•MINIMUM TIME•	4hrs
•ASCENT / GRADIENT•	1,445ft (440m) ▲▲▲
•LEVEL OF DIFFICULTY•	🚶 🚶 🚶
•PATHS•	Generally hard and rocky, some boggy patches on moorland top
•LANDSCAPE•	Steep hillsides with rocky outcrops and open moorland
•SUGGESTED MAP•	aqua3 OS Explorer OL1 Dark Peak
•START / FINISH•	Grid reference: SE 013036
•DOG FRIENDLINESS•	Mostly open sheep country subject to access agreements so on lead or close control at all times
•PARKING•	Car park below Dovestone Reservoir dam (pay-and-display at weekends)
•PUBLIC TOILETS•	By car park

BACKGROUND TO THE WALK

Around 130 years ago, as the demands of Manchester's industrial population grew, the need to supply the city with safe and sufficient drinking water became paramount. Inevitably the planners turned their attentions towards the Pennines, that formidable upland barrier that soaks up so much of northern England's rain. Before long a series of reservoirs sprung up across the hills that separated urban Lancashire and Yorkshire and, just as the counties' rivers and streams had previously been harnessed for the mills, now the moorlands were drained and the tiny Pennine valleys dammed to create artificial lakes. The first of the four reservoirs collectively known as Dovestones was Yeoman Hey, constructed in 1880, and followed by Greenfield in 1902. When Chew Reservoir was built, ten years later, it was the highest in Britain at around 1,600ft (488m). Dovestone Reservoir is the largest of the group and was completed in 1967.

Four Reservoirs
Today the four reservoirs supply drinking water to Oldham and communities in the Tame Valley. They are owned and run by United Utilities, who provide water to nearly 3 million people in North West England. In total the water company owns around 140,000 acres (56,700ha) of water-gathering land and actual reservoirs throughout the Peak District, Lake District and West Pennines. Here at Dovestones water collects in Chew Reservoir, high and remote on the top of the bleak moorland, before travelling via an underground pipe almost 1 mile (1.6km) long to emerge at an aqueduct at Ashway Gap, below Dean Rocks. Water is then held in the two main reservoirs in the valley bottom, Dovestone and Yeoman Hey, before being piped further down the valley for treatment at a large plant at Buckton Castle in Mossley. It's also used by a paper mill located below Dovestone Reservoir dam.

Recreation

United Utilities actively encourages certain types of recreation around its reservoirs. Swimming is forbidden, because of the deep water and outlet pipes that can cause dangerous undercurrents, but sailing and windsurfing take place on Dovestone Reservoir, with regular regattas. On the adjoining hillside there are two orienteering routes – look out for the small posts with coloured markings and numbers. The popular 2½-mile (4km) track around the shore of Dovestone Reservoir has been made suitable for wheelchair users, while the numerous paths and bridleways that explore the surrounding moors also include the Oldham Way. The course of this circular, 40-mile (64.3km) walking route around the borough of Oldham can be seen as you set off from Dovestone Reservoir. It runs high and straight across the hillside to the south on the route of a former steam tramway that was built 90 years ago to aid the construction of Chew Reservoir.

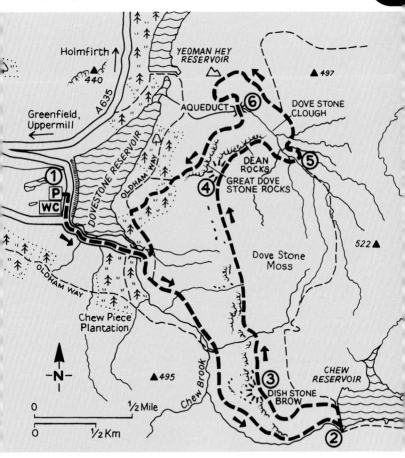

Walk 37 Directions

① From the car park walk up to the top of the **Dovestone Reservoir** dam and turn right, along the road past the **sailing club**. Where the plantation ends go straight on over a bridge and follow this private, vehicular track as it makes its way steadily up to the very top of the **Chew Valley**.

WHAT TO LOOK FOR ⓘ
As you stand on the edge of the moors above Dovestone Reservoir, taking in the splendid panorama westwards, a small but distinctively pointed hill a mile (1.6km) beyond the reservoir (and topped by a war memorial) tends to catch the eye. It's known as **Pots and Pans** and its odd-shaped rocks contain weathered holes that were once rumoured to have been specially deepened to hold the wine of well-to-do grouse shooters!

② When you reach **Chew Reservoir** turn left and walk along by the dam wall until just before it kinks right. With your back to the reservoir (and a sign warning of the dangers of deep water) drop down to the moorland and follow the very wide, straight track opposite that heads back towards the edge of the hillside. It first bears left, then swings back to the right, and soon becomes a thin path that weaves its way between the loose rocks around **Dish Stone Brow**.

③ With Dovestone Reservoir coming into view far below, continue along the high rim of the hillside past a series of rocky outcrops. If you occasionally lose sight of the path don't worry – just keep to the wide strip between the steep drop on your left and the banks of peaty bog on your right.

④ Nearing **Great Dove Stone Rocks** continue to follow the rocky edge as it swings back to the right. Beyond **Dean Rocks** is a clear path that winds its way around the head of a narrow valley known as **Dove Stone Clough**.

⑤ Cross the stream as it flows over a rocky shelf and, as you continue across the slope on the far side, the narrow path slowly begins to drop down the grassy hillside. Ignore a higher path towards a prominent stone memorial cross ahead. Soon the path curves steeply down to the left and there are numerous criss-crossing tracks through the long grass and bracken. If you are in any doubt then just aim for the unmistakable **aqueduct** below you, at the foot of **Dove Stone Clough**, and cross it by the high footbridge.

WHERE TO EAT AND DRINK ⓘ
On sunny weekends the occasional ice cream van is a welcome addition to Dovestones car park. Otherwise the nearest outlet is a pub called the **Clarence**, about a mile (1.6km) away in Greenfield, which serves food Tuesday–Sunday lunchtimes. For more choice you'll have to try the cafés and pubs of nearby Uppermill.

⑥ Walk along the path below the rock face on your left and across an area of slumped hillside littered with rock debris. Eventually the path joins a wide, grassy strip that gently leads down between fenced-off plantations of young conifers. Go through the gate and drop down the edge of the open field to reach the popular reservoir-side track. Turn left and follow this all the way back to the car park.

WHILE YOU'RE THERE ⓘ
A visit to **Saddleworth Museum and Art Gallery**, 2 miles (3.2km) from Dovestones on the High Street in Uppermill, is highly recommended. The former canalside woollen mill is stuffed full of curiosities and intriguing snippets of local history – from farming to brass bands, Roman soldiers to weaving mills. It's open daily and includes hands-on exhibits for children and constantly changing displays.

Standedge from Marsden

A classic moorland ramble on the ancient Rapes Highway.

•DISTANCE•	6½ miles (10.4km)
•MINIMUM TIME•	3hrs 30min
•ASCENT / GRADIENT•	900ft (375m) ▲▲▲
•LEVEL OF DIFFICULTY•	𝄡 𝄡 𝄡
•PATHS•	Old tracks and byways, canal tow path, 5 stiles
•LANDSCAPE•	Heather moorland
•SUGGESTED MAP•	aqua3 OS Explorer OL21 South Pennines
•START / FINISH•	Grid reference: SE 048117
•DOG FRIENDLINESS•	Keep under control where sheep graze on open moorland
•PARKING•	Free street parking in Marsden
•PUBLIC TOILETS•	Marsden, at start of walk

BACKGROUND TO THE WALK

Trans-Pennine travel has, until quite recently, been a hazardous business. Over the centuries many routes have been driven across the hills to link the industrial centres of West Yorkshire and Lancashire. Some paths were consolidated into paved causeways for packhorse traffic, before being upgraded to take vehicles. This track, linking the Colne Valley to the Lancashire towns of Rochdale and Milnrow, was known as the Rapes Highway.

The Standedge Tunnel

This was tough terrain for building a canal. When the Huddersfield Narrow Canal was cut, to provide a link between Huddersfield and Ashton-under-Lyne, there was one major obstacle for the canal builders to overcome. The gritstone bulk of Standedge straddled the county border. There was no way round; the canal had to go through. The Standedge Tunnel, extending 3 miles (4.8km) from Marsden to Diggle, was a monumental feat of engineering. Costly in every sense, it took 16 years to build and many navvies lost their lives. The result was the longest, highest and deepest canal tunnel in the country.

In an attempt to keep those costs down, the tunnel was cut as narrow as possible, which left no room for a tow path. Towing horses had to be led over the hills to the far end of the tunnel, near Diggle in Lancashire. The bargees had to negotiate Standedge Tunnel using their own muscle power alone. This method, known as 'legging', required them to lie on their backs and push with their feet against the sides and roof of the tunnel. This operation would typically take a back-breaking 4 hours; it would have been a great relief to see the proverbial light at the end of the tunnel. Closed to canal traffic for many years, the tunnel is currently being restored for recreational users (at least those with strong legs and backs).

In 1812 Marsden became the focus for the 'Luddite' rebellion against mechanisation in the textile industry. A secret group of croppers and weavers banded together to break up the new machinery which was appearing in local mills and which had been developed by local industrialists. The rebellion caused much consternation and eventually the army was despatched to restore order. Sixty men were put on trial in York for their part in the troubles; 17 of them were subsequently hanged.

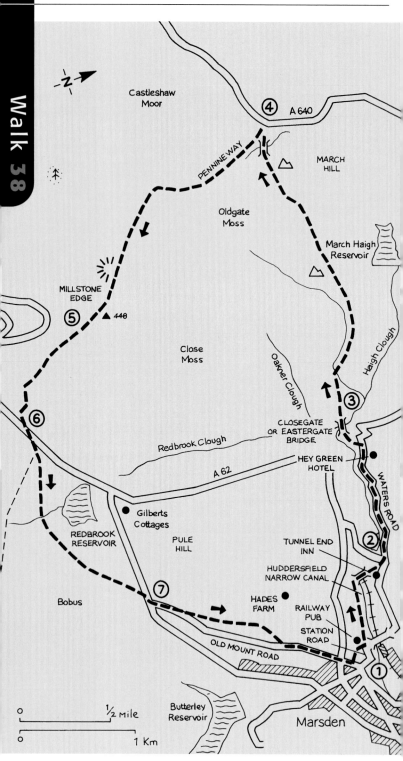

Walk 38

Castleshaw Moor

④ A 640

MARCH HILL

PENNINE WAY

Oldgate Moss

March Haigh Reservoir

MILLSTONE EDGE

⑤ ▲ 448

Close Moss

Oakner Clough

Haigh Clough

③

CLOSEGATE OR EASTERGATE BRIDGE

Redbrook Clough

⑥

A 62

HEY GREEN HOTEL

WATERS ROAD

Gilberts Cottages

REDBROOK RESERVOIR

PULE HILL

TUNNEL END INN

②

HUDDERSFIELD NARROW CANAL

Bobus

⑦

HADES FARM

RAILWAY PUB

STATION ROAD

OLD MOUNT ROAD

①

½ mile

1 Km

Butterley Reservoir

Marsden

Walk 38

Walk 38 Directions

① From the centre of **Marsden**, take **Station Road**, uphill. Between the **Railway** pub, and the station itself, go left along the tow path of the **Huddersfield Narrow Canal**. At **Tunnel End** – where both canal and train lines disappear into a tunnel through the hillside – cross the canal on a footbridge, and walk up a track to the **Tunnel End Inn**.

② Walk left along **Waters Road**. Keep straight ahead after ½ mile (800m), at the entrance to the **Hey Green Hotel**.100yds (91m) further on, bear left, just before a cottage, on to a footpath. The path takes you across **Closegate Bridge**, known locally as **Eastergate Bridge**, where two becks meet.

WHAT TO LOOK FOR ⓘ

In spring and early summer, listen out for a cuckoo. If an old story is to be believed, the people of Marsden realised that when the **cuckoo** arrived, so did the sunshine. They tried to keep spring forever, by building a tower around the cuckoo. As the last stones were about to be laid, however, the cuckoo flew away. The good folk of Marsden use the joke against themselves, and now celebrate Cuckoo Day in April each year.

---

③ Keep right, following the right-hand beck for about 100yds (91m), when the path bears left, up a steep side-valley. The path levels off at the top and then bears slightly right, towards the rounded prominence of **March Hill**. Your route across moorland is soon marked by a series of waymarker stones, though your way ahead is unmistakable. After a few ups and downs, the path rises steeply uphill, before descending towards the A640.

④ Just before you reach the road, take a wooden bridge over a little beck and follow a **Pennine Way** sign on a track that bears acute left. Take this well-maintained gravel track uphill. After a few minutes you follow the contours of **Millstone Edge**, a rocky ridge that offers panoramic views into **East Lancashire**. Just before the trig point is a plaque commemorating Amon Wrigley, a local poet.

⑤ Your route is downhill from here. Take a succession of stiles in walls and fences before going left on an unmade track that leads down to the A62, where a car park overlooks **Brunclough Reservoir**.

⑥ Cross the road and take steps up to the left of the car park, signed '**Pennine Way**', to access a good track, soon revealing views to the left of **Redbrook Reservoir** and **Pule Hill** beyond. At a marker stone the **Pennine Way** bears right. But your route – having made a small detour to cross a tiny beck – is to continue along the track. It gradually sweeps left, around the slopes of **Pule Hill**, to reach a road.

⑦ Turn right, along the road, but then immediately left, up **Old Mount Road**. After 100yds (91m), bear left again, up a stony track signed to **Hades** farm. After ½ mile (800m), take a path to the right, that accompanies a wall, to rejoin **Old Mount Road**. Follow the road downhill to arrive back in **Marsden**.

WHERE TO EAT AND DRINK ⓘ

Marsden is not short of characterful pubs, but the two most convenient watering holes on this walk are the **Railway** and the **Tunnel End Inn** (near the railway station and Tunnel End, respectively and predictably).

Walk 39

A Colourful Circuit of Norland Moor

Awash with colour in late summer, Norland Moor is an island of heather moorland in the midst of busy milltowns.

•DISTANCE•	5 miles (8km)
•MINIMUM TIME•	2hrs 30min
•ASCENT / GRADIENT•	328ft (100m) ▲ ▲ ▲
•LEVEL OF DIFFICULTY•	🚶 🚶 🚶
•PATHS•	Good moorland paths and tracks, 1 stile
•LANDSCAPE•	Heather moor and woodland
•SUGGESTED MAP•	aqua3 OS Outdoor Leisure 21 South Pennines
•START / FINISH•	Grid reference: SE 055218
•DOG FRIENDLINESS•	Dogs can roam off lead, though watch for grazing sheep
•PARKING•	Small public car park opposite Moorcock Inn, on unclassified road immediately south of Sowerby Bridge
•PUBLIC TOILETS•	None on route

BACKGROUND TO THE WALK

Norland Moor and North Dean Woods are close to the start of the Calderdale Way, a 50-mile (80-km) circuit of the borough of Calderdale. There are panoramic views straight away, as the waymarked walk accompanies the edge of Norland Moor. The route was inaugurated during the 1970s to link some of the best Pennine landscapes and historical sites – moors, mills, gritstone outcrops, wooded cloughs, hand-weaving hamlets and industrial towns – into an invigorating walk.

Norland Moor

Norland Moor is a 253-acre (102-ha) tract of heather moorland overlooking Sowerby Bridge and both the Calder and Ryburn valleys. Criss-crossed by paths, it is popular with local walkers; riven by old quarry workings, it is a reminder that here in West Yorkshire you are seldom far from a site of industry. Originally a part of the Savile estates, the moor was bought for £250 after a public appeal in 1932. It still has the status of a common. Part of the attraction is to find such splendid walking country so close to the busy towns in the valley.

Ladstone Rock is a gritstone outcrop with a distinctive profile that stares out over the Ryburn Valley from the edge of Norland Moor. If you can believe the stories, human sacrifices were carried out on Ladstone Rock by blood-thirsty druids, and convicted witches were thrown off it. The name may derive from Celtic roots, meaning to cut or to kill. There is a tradition in the South Pennines of carving inspirational quotations into such rocks. And here on Ladstone Rock, amongst the names, dates and expressions of undying love, is a small metal plaque inscribed with a short psalm from the Bible.

Wainhouse Tower

As you leave the nature reserve of North Dean Woods behind, you get good views across the valley to Sowerby Bridge and the outskirts of Halifax. Dominating the view is a curious edifice known as Wainhouse Tower (and also, tellingly, as Wainhouse Folly). It was built by John Wainhouse, who had inherited his uncle's dyeworks. His first plan was to build a tall chimney that would help to disperse the noxious fumes from the dyeworks. But then he decided to add a spiral staircase, inside the chimney, leading up to an ornate viewing platform at the top. By the time the tower was actually built, in the 1870s, the original purpose seems to have been forgotten. To climb to the full height of the tower, 253 ft (77m), you need to tackle more than 400 steps. The tower is opened up to the public, but on just a few occasions each year – generally on bank holidays. If Wainhouse failed to make a chimney, then he succeeded in creating a distinctive landmark.

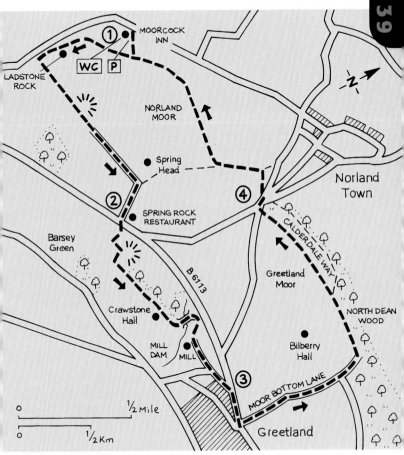

Walk 39 Directions

① Walk uphill from the **Moorcock Inn**, bearing right near the top to follow a clear path along the edge of **Norland Moor**. Enjoy expansive views across the **Calder Valley** as you pass the gritstone outcrop

known as **Ladstone Rock**. Keep straight ahead, now on a more substantial track which descends almost to a road. Bear left at a **Calderdale Way** sign, on a faint path uphill. Head for the wall at the top of the hill. Follow the wall to the left; then turn right, still following the wall, to walk on a

> **WHERE TO EAT AND DRINK** ℹ️
> Your best choice is the **Moorcock Inn**, close to where you parked. This is a popular meeting place for the local walking and rambling clubs – either before their walk on the moors or after.

path that becomes enclosed between walls as you leave the open moorland behind. At a fork of paths, keep straight ahead before going right, along a farm track to emerge at the **Spring Rock Restaurant**.

② Cross the road and continue on the narrowest of walled paths opposite the restaurant. Extensive views open up as the path goes right, down stone steps. Where the walled path ends, go left on a grassy path. Keep left of cottages on a good track. When you meet a fork of tracks, keep right, downhill, and immediately take a path that bears slightly to the left, into a small wood. The path soon descends to cross a stream on a stone-slab bridge, and bears right uphill to meet a walled track. Take the narrow path (not the walled track), which bears ahead and slightly left to skirts the walls of a house and garden before joining the road (B6113) between two houses.

③ Walk right, along the road, for 150yds (138m) and take a good track on the left, **Moor Bottom**

> **WHILE YOU'RE THERE** ℹ️
> After years of dereliction, the canal marina in **Sowerby Bridge** is slowly coming back to life. The centre of town was closed off to traffic for almost a year, while a filled-in section of canal was opened up to boats once again. This was made possible by building what is now – at 15ft (more than 5m) – the deepest canal lock in the country.

Lane. Continue along this ruler-straight track, ignoring side-turnings, to enter **North Dean Wood** (from here you follow signs and arrows for the **Calderdale Way**). Keep left where the path forks to walk along the left-hand edge of the woodland, following a wall. Go uphill, over a stile, and on to a field path, still keeping the wood to your right. Join a track that soon meets a minor road. Go right, down to a sharp right-hand bend.

> **WHAT TO LOOK FOR** ℹ️
> The plateau of Norland Moor, overlooking Sowerby Bridge and the Calder Valley, is a particular delight in late summer, when the **heather** is in purple flower. Although we now consider heather to be the natural plant to grow on these moors, its introduction is relatively recent. Heather will not grow in the shade, and so it was not until all the trees had been cleared off these hills by early settlers that it really took a hold. You should also look for the bitter-sweet tasting bilberry, which is a favourite with grazing sheep around the end of June, and the less palatable (and mildly poisonous) crowberries, which cluster on rockier ground.

④ From here you bear left, following the **Calderdale Way** sign, on a stony track across **Norland Moor**. As you pass a pylon, take a path that keeps just to the right of the line of pylons ahead. You can soon take one of a choice of paths to the right, to reach the well-defined edge of **Norland Moor** once again, and back to your car.

Jumble Hole and Colden Clough

Textile history from cottage industry to the mills of bustling Hebden Bridge.

•DISTANCE•	5½ miles (8.8km)
•MINIMUM TIME•	3hrs
•ASCENT / GRADIENT•	722ft (220m) ▲▲▲
•LEVEL OF DIFFICULTY•	🚶🚶 🚶🚶 🚶
•PATHS•	Good paths, 13 stiles
•LANDSCAPE•	Steep-sided valleys, fields and woodland
•SUGGESTED MAP•	aqua3 OS Outdoor Leisure 21 South Pennines
•START / FINISH•	Grid reference: SD 992272
•DOG FRIENDLINESS•	Good most of the way, but livestock in upland fields
•PARKING•	Pay-and-display car parks in Hebden Bridge
•PUBLIC TOILETS•	Hebden Bridge and Heptonstall

BACKGROUND TO THE WALK

This walk links the little town of Hebden Bridge with the old hand-weaving village of Heptonstall, using sections of a waymarked walk, the Calderdale Way. The hill village of Heptonstall is by far the older settlement and was, in its time, an important centre of the textile trade. A cursory look at a map shows Heptonstall to be at the hub of a complex network of old trackways, mostly used by packhorse trains carrying wool and cotton. And Heptonstall's Cloth Hall, where cloth was bought and sold, dates back to the 16th century. At this time Hebden Bridge was little more than a river crossing on an old packhorse causey.

Wheels of Industry

Heptonstall's importance came at the time when textiles were, literally, a cottage industry, with spinning and weaving being undertaken in isolated farmhouses. When the processes began to be mechanised, during the Industrial Revolution, Heptonstall, with no running water to power the waterwheels, was left high and dry. As soon as spinning and weaving developed on a truly industrial scale, communities sprang up wherever there was a ready supply of running water. So the town of Hebden Bridge was established in the valley, at the meeting of two rivers: the Calder and Hebden Water. The handsome 16th-century packhorse bridge that gives the town its name still spans Hebden Water.

At one time there were more than 30 mills in Hebden Bridge, their tall chimneys belching thick smoke into the Calder Valley. It used to be said that the only time you could see the town from the surrounding hills was during Wakes Week, the mill-hands' traditional holiday. The town's speciality was cotton: mostly hard-wearing fustian and corduroy. With Hebden Bridge being hemmed in by hills, and the mills occupying much of the available land on the valley bottom, the workers' houses had to be built up the steep slopes. An ingenious solution to the problem was to build 'top and bottom' houses, one dwelling on top of another. They can be viewed to best effect on the last leg of the walk, which offers a stunning birds-eye view over the town. Few looms clatter today and Hebden Bridge has reinvented itself as the 'capital' of Upper Calderdale, as a place to enjoy a day out. The town is known for its excellent walking country, bohemian population, trips along the Rochdale Canal by horse-drawn narrowboats and its summer arts festival. Jumble Hole Clough is a typical South Pennine steep-sided, wooded valley. Though a tranquil scene today, this little valley was once a centre of industry, with four mills exploiting the fast-flowing beck as it makes its way down to join the River Calder. You can see remains of all these mills, and some of their mill ponds, on this walk; but the most intriguing relic is Staups Mill, now an evocative ruin, near the top of Jumble Hole Clough.

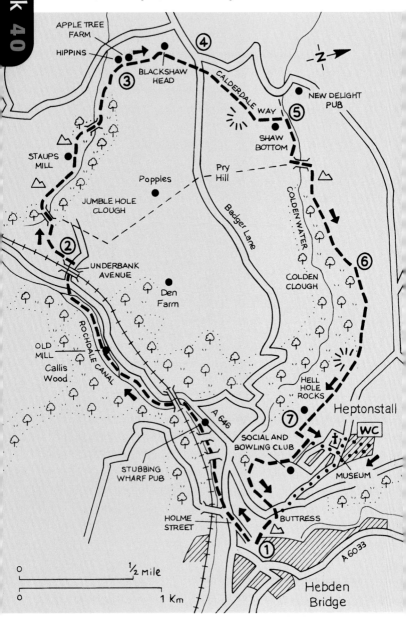

Walk 40 Directions

① From the centre of **Hebden Bridge**, walk along **Holme Street** to the **Rochdale Canal**. Go right to follow the tow path beneath two bridges, past the **Stubbing Wharf** pub and beneath a railway bridge. Beyond the bridge the canal broadens; 200yds (183m) further on and before the next bridge, bear right and join a track right, to the A646.

② Cross the road and bear right for just 75yds (68m) to take **Underbank Avenue**, on the left, through an arch. Bear left again, past houses, to where another road comes through the viaduct. Go right on a track past a mill, and follow the beck up into the woodland of **Jumble Hole Clough**. Beyond a ruined mill, leave the track and bear left to cross the beck. Beyond a hairpin bend, climb steeply, passing a dam. When the track wheels left, keep ahead, now above the beck. Take a gate and cross the bottom of a field, to re-enter woodland. Keep ahead uphill, to a gap in a fence. Walk downhill, past the ruins of **Staups Mill**, then steeply up to cross a bridge. Take steps and cross a field to a waymark. Keep left, following a wall to a gate in front of **Hippins**.

③ Join the **Calderdale Way**, bearing right up a track between farm buildings to a stile. Follow a path to the next stile; then between a fence and a wall. Cross the track to **Apple Tree Farm**, to follow a line of causeway stones across three more stiles, passing to the right of a cottage. Cross the field to a gate at the right corner, then follow a causeway over a stile, and along a track to **Blackshaw Head**.

④ Go right, along the road, for 20yds (18m), to take a gate on the left. Bear half right across the field to a stile, then follow the right edge of the next field. Cross four more fields, and stiles, to a gate. Go left down a path, to **Shaw Bottom**. Keep left of the house to a metalled track.

⑤ Go right, along the track (or left for the **New Delight** pub). When the track bears left, keep ahead on a stony track. Look out for a small marker post; go left here, steeply down steps, and cross **Colden Water** on a stone bridge. Climb up the other side, to follow a causeway to the right, at the top of woodland. At the second stile bear slightly left to keep following the causeway stones; your route is clear, through gates and stiles, as **Heptonstall** comes into view. Keep right at a crossing of tracks, passing to the left of a house. Keep straight ahead, on a walled path downhill, at the next crossing of tracks, by a bench. Keep left at the next fork to meet a road.

⑥ Go left here, uphill; just before the road bears left, take a gap in the wall to the right. From here your path meanders through woodland (it's a bit of a scramble in places). Emerge from the woodland, and follow a wall to **Hell Hole Rocks**.

⑦ Bear left at a wall-end, and cross an access road. At the junction turn right to the **Social and Bowling Club**. Go right, on a walled path and follow the wall to your left, downhill, soon through a spur of woodland and on to a track round to the left. Past houses you come to a road junction. Go left for 50yds (46m) and take the paved track right. This is the **Buttress**, taking you steeply down into **Hebden Bridge**.

The Mines of Greenhow and Bewerley Moor

Through a landscape of lead mining, from one of Yorkshire's highest villages.

•DISTANCE•	5¾ miles (9.2km)
•MINIMUM TIME•	2hrs 30min
•ASCENT / GRADIENT•	1,181ft (360m) ▲▲▲
•LEVEL OF DIFFICULTY•	👫 👫 👫
•PATHS•	Field and moorland paths and tracks, 3 stiles
•LANDSCAPE•	Moorland and valley, scarred by fascinating remains of the lead mining industry
•SUGGESTED MAP•	aqua3 OS Explorer 298 Nidderdale
•START / FINISH•	Grid reference: SE 114642
•DOG FRIENDLINESS•	Dogs can be off lead for much of the route
•PARKING•	Car park by Miners Arms
•PUBLIC TOILETS•	None on route

BACKGROUND TO THE WALK

It is a long haul from Pateley Bridge up Greenhow Hill to the village of Greenhow, one of the highest in Yorkshire, at around 1,300ft (396m) above sea level. Until the early 17th century this was all bleak and barren moorland. When lead mining on a significant scale developed in the area in the 1600s, a settlement was established here, though most of the surviving buildings are late 18th and 19th century. Many of the cottages also have a small piece of attached farmland, for the miners were also farmers, neither occupation alone giving them a stable income or livelihood. In a way typical of such mining villages, the church and the pub – the Miners Arms, of course – are at the very centre.

Romans and Monks

Romans are the first known miners of Greenhow, though there is said to be some evidence of even earlier activity, as far back as the Bronze Age. The Romans had a camp near Pateley Bridge, and ingots of lead – called 'pigs' – have been found nearby, dating from the 1st century AD. In the Middle Ages lead from Yorkshire became important for roofing castles and cathedrals – it is said that it was even used in Jerusalem. Production was governed by the major landowners, the monasteries, and some, like Fountains and Byland, became rich from selling charters for mining and from royalties. After the monasteries were dissolved, the new landowners wanted to exploit their mineral rights, and encouraged many small-scale enterprises in return for a share of the profits.

As you leave Greenhow and begin to descend into the valley of the Gill Beck, you pass through the remains of the Cockhill Mine. It is still possible to make out the dressing floor, where the lead ore was separated from the waste rock and other minerals, and the location of the smelt works, where the ore was processed. Beyond, by the Ashfold Side Beck, were the Merryfield Mines and, where the route crosses the beck, there are extensive remains of the Prosperous Smelt Mill. All these mines were active in the middle of the 19th century, and some had a brief resurgence in the mid 20th.

Besides the Lead

Coldstones Quarry, opposite you when you've reached the main road past Coldstones Farm, opened about 1900. It produces limestone – almost 1 million tonnes a year. Around Greenhow the limestone layers are particularly deep, allowing large blocks to be cut. Across it run two mineral veins, called Garnet Vein and Sun Vein, both of which have been mined in the past for lead and (later) for fluorite. Other minerals found in smaller quantities in the rock here are barite, calcite and galena, as well as crystals of cerrusite, anglesite and occasionally quartz.

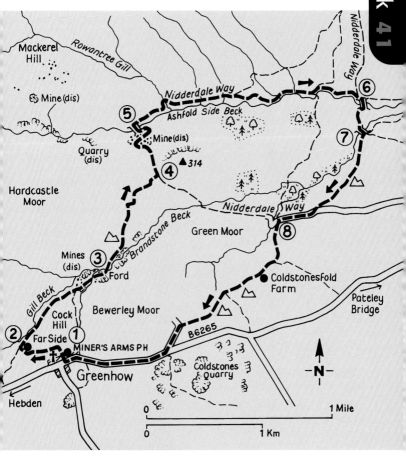

Walk 41 Directions

① Turn right out of the car park. After about 100yds (91m), just after a converted chapel, take a lane to the right. At the junction go left and follow the lane to a cattle grid and through a gate. Curve right, round behind the farmhouse.

② Follow the track downhill into the valley of **Gill Beck** and then **Brandstone Beck**, where there are the extensive remains of lead mining activity. Where the track swings left, go ahead down the valley to reach the main track near a concrete building. Go right of the building and just beyond go ahead down the valley to the ford.

WHILE YOU'RE THERE ⓘ

Nearby **Stump Cross Caverns** can take you into the underground world below Greenhow. The limestone cave system was discovered in the middle of the 19th century. You can visit a succession of caves with plenty of stalagmites and stalactites, many with fanciful names, where ancient animal bones, including those of the wolverine, have been discovered. It is open daily from mid-March to mid-November.

③ Cross and follow the obvious track up the hill. Go over a stile beside a gate by trees then, 100yds (91m) beyond, take another stile on the right. Follow the track towards the farm, going left between stone walls, and descend to another stile on to a track.

④ Turn left and go through a waymarked gateway. By a spoil heap follow the track to the right and downhill. Veer slightly left, past an iron cogwheel, to cross **Ashfold Side Beck** on a concrete causeway to a gate.

⑤ Follow the bridleway sign to the right and climb the hill, to a **Nidderdale Way** sign, where you turn right along the track to a gate. Wind round the head of a valley through two gateways and over three cattle grids. Just beyond the third, go through a metal gate to the right and over the bridge.

⑥ Go ahead then bear left to another gate and follow the track uphill and left to a wall. Turn right at the end of the wall along a lane between stone walls. Continue along the track to a gate and cross a footbridge.

⑦ Turn right through a gate and follow the track uphill, passing through another gate. Turn left at another track, making towards the farmhouse, but bear right across the grass to meet a metalled lane. Turn right and follow the lane over a cattle grid.

⑧ 100yds (91m) beyond the farm on the right, turn left up a signed footpath. After a cattle grid turn right and follow the track, passing through a gate. At **Coldstonesfold Farm** turn right and follow the track uphill through three gates on to a metalled lane. Turn left and go uphill to meet the main road. Turn right to return to the **Miner's Arms**.

WHERE TO EAT AND DRINK ⓘ

The **Miner's Arms** in Greenhow offers meals and bar snacks, as well as good local beer. **Stump Cross Caverns** has a tea room. Pateley Bridge is well served with hotels, pubs, restaurants and tea rooms. **Apothecary's House** serves light lunches and teas. **Grassfields Country House Hotel** in Low Wath Road has both a restaurant and a bistro in an elegant Georgian mansion.

WHAT TO LOOK FOR ⓘ

Although limestone is the bedrock of the upper part of Greenhow Hill, in the valleys to the east it is the characteristic **millstone grit** that forms the landscape. A carboniferous sandstone, millstone grit is the typical local building material, and most of Greenhow village's houses are made from it. You can recognise it by the large, shiny grains of quartz embedded in it. It's a very hard stone, so, unlike limestone, does not carve easily; fine detail is not something you would expect on a millstone grit building. As its name suggests, however, its hardness made it ideal for millstones. Nidderdale Marble, a dark, metamorphosed limestone that takes a high polish, was quarried in the area, too. It was used in local churches – including Fountains Abbey – for thin decorative columns.

The Iron Valley of Rosedale

Reminders of former industry are all around you on this route near Rosedale Abbey.

•DISTANCE•	3½ miles (5.7km)
•MINIMUM TIME•	1hr 30min
•ASCENT / GRADIENT•	558ft (170m) ▲▲▲
•LEVEL OF DIFFICULTY•	🏃🏃 🏃🏃 🏃🏃
•PATHS•	Mostly field paths and tracks, 11 stiles
•LANDSCAPE•	Quiet valley and hillside farmland, with reminders of the iron industry
•SUGGESTED MAP•	aqua3 OS Outdoor Leisure 26 North York Moors – Western
•START / FINISH•	Grid reference: SE 708964
•DOG FRIENDLINESS•	Dogs should be on leads
•PARKING•	Roadside parking, with care, in Thorgill
•PUBLIC TOILETS•	None on route

BACKGROUND TO THE WALK

Rosedale is a quiet and peaceful valley that pushes north west into the heart of the North York Moors. The village of Rosedale Abbey gets its name from the former Cistercian nunnery of which only the angle of a wall remains. Yet little more than 100 years ago the village had a population ten times its present size. The reason was the discovery of ironstone in the hills in the mid 1850s. From 1856 onwards commercial exploitation began, new rows of cottages were built for the miners and, as one of the villagers wrote in 1869, 'The ground is hollow for many a mile underground… It's like a little city now but is a regular slaughter place. Both men and horses are getting killed and lamed every day.'

The East Mines
The dramatic remains of the Rosedale East Mines, which opened in 1865, can be seen during much of the walk. Now being cared for by the National Park Authority with help from English Heritage, they are a testament to the size of the mining operations. The long range of huge arches is the remains of the calcining kilns, where the ironstone was roasted to eliminate impurities and reduce its weight. They operated until 1879, when the owner, the Rosedale and Ferryhill Mining Company, collapsed, but resumed in 1881. The West Mines across the valley had stopped work by 1890, but the East Mines struggled on, burdened by rising costs, until the General Strike of 1926, which effectively killed them off.

The Iron Way
The mined iron ore from Rosedale was taken by rail from the mines and over the moorland to Ingleby, where it was lowered down the northern edge of the moors by tramway on the 1-in-5 gradient Ingleby Incline. The line had reached Rosedale in 1861, and the branch to the East Mines was opened in 1865. As many as 15 loaded wagons at a time were steam hauled round the top of Rosedale. The line closed in September 1928, and the last load was hauled down Ingleby Incline in June the following year. The track bed is now open for walkers to enjoy its engineered gradients.

The Vanished Chimney

For more than a century the village of Rosedale Abbey was dominated by an industrial chimney, more than 100ft (30m) tall. One of the steepest public roads in the country went past it to reach the heights of Spaunton Moor. The road is still there, but the chimney was demolished in 1972, a victim of the inability to raise the £6,000 needed to preserve it – and symptomatic of the public attitude to industrial archaeology that prevailed at the time.

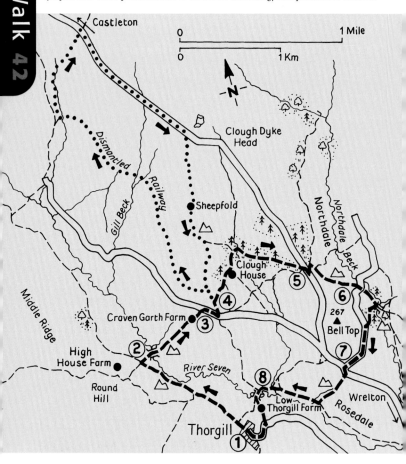

Walk 42 **Directions**

① From your parking place in the hamlet of **Thorgill**, continue up the lane, pass a public bridleway sign and go through a metal gate. Follow the track, going through a wooden gate and beginning to rise. Almost opposite a farmhouse on the left, go right over a wooden stile beside a gate.

② Walk down the slope to pass over the stream on a gated footbridge, then turn slightly left to go uphill on the opposite bank beside the trees. Continue through a gate into the field and walk ahead, going over a stile then through a metal gate into the yard of **Craven Garth Farm**. Go through another gateway and pass between the buildings to reach **Daleside Road**, a metalled country lane.

Walk 42

③ Turn right; just before reaching the cottage, turn left up a track by the parish notice board. A little way up the track look for a stile beside the gate to **Clough House**.

④ Go over the stile and follow the track downhill towards the wood, passing around the garden of **Clough House** and up to a stile, where you turn right and follow the waymarked path through the wood to reach a stile on to a road.

⑤ Turn right, then go left through a gate at a bridleway sign. Go down the grassy path to meet a level track. Turn left. Just before a gate, go right, following the bridleway sign. Continue downhill to reach a ladder stile, and go straight ahead across the field to reach a gateway on to a road by a bridleway sign.

⑥ Cross the road and continue ahead. After passing through a gateway, turn right at the footpath sign before the bridge. The track climbs steeply to a road. Turn left along the road to a T-junction.

⑦ Turn left. Opposite the **Bell End Farm** sign turn right through a gate, and continue down the field to a stile. The path bends and descends steeply. On reaching a fence, turn sharp right to go over a boardwalk and through a waymarked gate.

WHILE YOU'RE THERE

Take the road north from Rosedale Abbey to Rosedale Head, where you will find **Young Ralph Cross**, symbol of the North York Moors National Park. A little way to the west is **Old Ralph**. Young Ralph is 18th century, replacing one on the site from at least 1200. It is said to have been put up by a farmer from Danby called Ralph who found a dead traveller on the spot. Old Ralph, on the highest part of Blakey Ridge, is possibly 11th century, and is said to be named after Auld Ralph of Rosedale, a herdsman employed by Guisborough Priory.

Follow the path over two stiles. Turn left down the track, which passes though a gateway, and go straight on.

⑧ Just beyond a gate, go left, following the stream, to cross a footbridge with stiles at each end. Follow the footpath uphill towards the farm buildings. Follow the waymarks through the buildings and up the farm track to reach a lane. Turn right and go back to the car parking place.

WHERE TO EAT AND DRINK

The **Milburn Arms Hotel** in Rosedale Abbey offers high-class dining in its Priory Restaurant as well as meals in the beamed bar. The **Abbey Tea Rooms** provides coffee, light lunches and cream teas from Easter to the end of October.

WHAT TO LOOK FOR

Looming over Thorgill at the start of the walk, and visible across the valley from most of the walk, is the bulk of **Blakey Rigg**, one of the most prominent of the Moors' heights, which divides Rosedale and Farndale. The Hutton-le-Hole to Castleton road follows the ridge's top for most of its length, and there are superb views from it. The Lion Inn is one of the most popular pubs in the area – and one of the most isolated. The Rigg is also known as a landmark on the Lyke Wake Walk across the Moors, celebrated in the *Lyke Wake Dirge* starting 'This aye night', set by Benjamin Britten. The walk follows the route that corpses were taken for burial. Those who believe in the existence of ley lines – those channels of mystical power that criss-cross the country – reckon that Blakey Rigg is the focus for several of them.

Walk 43

A Whirl Around Whorlton and Swainby

From the once-industrial village of Swainby, a walk with fine views from the Moors and a taste of history in Whorlton.

•DISTANCE•	6 miles (9.7km)
•MINIMUM TIME•	2hrs 30min
•ASCENT / GRADIENT•	1,098ft (335m) ▲▲▲
•LEVEL OF DIFFICULTY•	🚶🚶 🚶🚶 🚶
•PATHS•	Tracks and moorland paths, lots of bracken, 11 stiles
•LANDSCAPE•	Farmland and moorland, with some woodland
•SUGGESTED MAP•	aqua3 OS Outdoor Leisure 26 North York Moors – Western
•START / FINISH•	Grid reference: NZ 477020
•DOG FRIENDLINESS•	Can be off lead on moorland and in woodland
•PARKING•	Roadside parking in Swainby village
•PUBLIC TOILETS•	None on route

BACKGROUND TO THE WALK

The charming and peaceful village street of Swainby, divided by its tree-lined stream, gives few hints of its dramatic past. It owes its existence to tragedy – the coming of plague – the Black Death – in the 14th century, when the inhabitants of the original village, just up the hill at Whorlton, deserted their homes and moved here. There may already have been a few houses here as Swainby means the village of the land workers, and is recorded in the 13th century. In the 19th century Swainby was shocked out of its peaceful, rural existence by the opening of the ironstone mines in Scugdale. The village took on many of the aspects of an American frontier town, becoming full of miners and their equipment, and awash with their smoke and clatter.

Jet Propelled

As well as ironstone, jet was mined in the Swainby area in the 19th century, including on Whorl Hill, which you will walk around. Most of the jet pits were small, employing no more than a dozen men, but they could be very profitable, especially during the boom time for jet, encouraged by the example of Queen Victoria's black mourning jewellery. Like coal, jet is fossilised wood. It comes in two types, hard and soft; hard jet was probably formed in sea water and soft jet in fresh water. It has been prized for more than 3,000 years, and was known to the Celts as Freya's Tears. Because it is easy to work and takes a fine polish, jet workshops could turn out large quantities of jewellery relatively quickly. Although some jet objects are still made, especially in Whitby, the industry had virtually died out by the 1920s.

Church and Castle

The path from Whorl Hill takes us into the deserted village of Whorlton. Little survived its abandonment after the Black Death except the church and the castle, both now partially ruined. On any but a sunny day, Holy Cross Church can be a disturbing place, with its avenue of yew trees leading to the arches of the nave, now open to the skies. The chancel is roofed, and a flap in the doorway allows you to look inside to see a fine early 14th-century oak figure of a knight. It is probably Nicholas, Lord Maynell, who fought with Edward I in Wales and hunted in the woods here. The gatehouse of the Maynell's castle, just along the road, is the only substantial part left. It was built at the end of the 14th century, and was besieged 250 years later during the Civil War. You can still see the marks of cannon balls from the Parliamentarians' guns on the walls. East of the castle, which occupied more than 6 acres (2.4 ha), are further earthworks, which protected the fortified village.

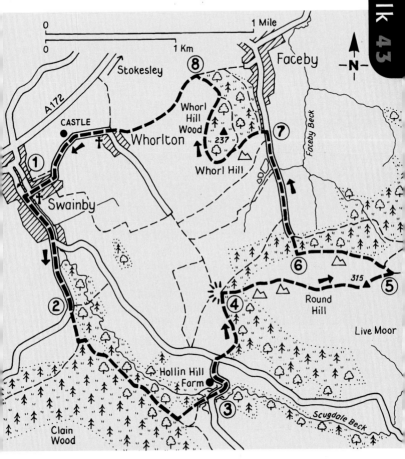

Walk 43 **Directions**

① With the church on your left, walk down the village street to the right of the stream. Continue past a sign 'Unsuitable for Coaches' and straight ahead uphill. As the road bends to the right, follow the bridleway sign to **Scugdale**, up the track ahead.

② Go through two gates, turning left after the second to join the waymarks for the the **Cleveland Way** National Trail. Walk through the woodland, turning left, just after a bench, down to a stile. The footpath goes downhill across the fields to another gate. Cross the stream on the footbridge to reach a lane, with another footbridge, over **Scugdale Beck**.

WHILE YOU'RE THERE ⓘ
Spend a moment of solitude at nearby **Mount Grace Priory**, the best preserved of England's charterhouses – communities of Carthusian monks. There's a reconstructed monk's cell showing how they lived as hermits, coming together rarely except for services in the church. Their isolation was such that even their meals were served through an L-shaped hatch so they couldn't see who brought them.

③ Follow the lane past **Hollin Hill Farm** to a T-junction with telephone and post boxes. Cross the lane and go through a **Cleveland Way** signed gate. Walk up the path beside woodland to a gate with a stile beside it (there's a view of the valley from this ridge).

④ The path turns right to a stile and goes on to a paved track in the wood. Go straight ahead at a crossing track to another stile, and continue to follow the paved path on to the heather moorland. After the first summit, the path descends beyond a cairn into a dip. After the paved path ends, look out for a narrow path off to the left, down through the heather.

⑤ After about 100yds (91m) you will reach a concrete post where the path forks. Take the left fork and follow the path down the gully to a fence beside a wall. Turn left,

forking left again down another gully to a signpost by a wall and fence. Follow the sign left and go over a spoil heap to reach a gate on your right.

⑥ Through the gate, go straight down the hill through woodland. At the bottom cross a stile by a gate and go down the lane. Just past a drive, where woodland begins, take a footpath over two stiles.

⑦ Walk up through the woodland on to a grassy track. Turn left, and left again at another track. At a T-junction, turn left again and follow the track downhill to a stile. Go straight ahead through a waymarked gateway.

WHERE TO EAT AND DRINK ⓘ
The **Blackmith's Arms** in Swainby, established in 1775, offers good beer and an extensive menu – though it no longer offers to shoe your horse. The **Black Horse** in the High Street is also noted for its beer.

⑧ Go over a stile beside a gate and follow the track along the hillside. Over a stile with steps beyond, turn left at the bottom and follow the field edge. Go over a waymarked stile by a gate and along the field. Walk along the field to a gate at the end, then follow the metalled lane past **Whorlton church** and castle back to **Swainby** village.

WHAT TO LOOK FOR ⓘ
From the highest part of the walk, which takes you up on to the northern edge of the North York Moors plateau, you are rewarded with extensive northward views over the vast industrial complexes surrounding **Middlesbrough**. It was the production of iron from the hills which really put Middlesbrough on the map; it had a population of just 40 in 1829, 7,600 in 1851, when the first blast furnace opened, and 20,000 nine years later. Prime Minister Gladstone called the town 'an infant Hercules'. Beyond the River Tees, the area of **Seal Sands** is home to an oil refinery and chemical works. It's the terminal of the 220 mile (352km) pipeline bringing oil and gas from the Ekofisk field in the North Sea. If you are on the hills at dawn or dusk, you may see the flare stacks glowing on the skyline.

Industrial Rookhope

The lead mining relics in this fascinating area inspired a 20th-century poet.

·DISTANCE·	5¼ miles (8.4km)
·MINIMUM TIME·	2hrs
·ASCENT / GRADIENT·	508ft (155m) ▲▲▲
·LEVEL OF DIFFICULTY·	🕴🕴 🕴🕴 🕴
·PATHS·	Tracks and field paths, one steep climb. Use former railway tracks as embankment may be unstable in places
·LANDSCAPE·	Former lead mining area with reminders of industrial past
·SUGGESTED MAP·	aqua3 OS Explorer 307 Consett & Derwent Reservoir
·START / FINISH·	Grid reference: NY 924430
·DOG FRIENDLINESS·	Can be off lead on much of trackbed
·PARKING·	Parking area beside Rookhope Arch, west of village
·PUBLIC TOILETS·	None on route

BACKGROUND TO THE WALK

Rookhope – its name means 'valley of the rooks' – is today a small, remote Weardale village. But it has a long and fascinating history. By 1153, when King Stephen granted a licence to mine for lead and iron, it was known as Rykhup. In the 14th century the local farmers combined agriculture with searching out the lead on the stream banks. The Rookhope farmers were generally free from the cattle raids that plagued their counterparts further north, but a famous raid of 1569 into Weardale ended with the raiders cornered in the Rookhope Valley, where a pitched battle resulted in victory for the Weardale men. Their exploits were recorded in the 24-verse ballad *Rookhope Ryde*.

A Bustling Town

Nineteenth-century Rookhope was a great contrast to the rest of its history. Under the influence of the Blackett family, the Weardale Iron Company and then the Weardale Lead Company, Rookhope became a bustling, noisy, industrial town, dedicated to winning minerals out of the ground in the surrounding hills. In its heyday its population approached 1,000, with ten shops, several churches and chapels, an Institute and generous sports fields. The mine owners maintained a paternalistic but benevolent eye on their workforce. There were still mines operating in the Rookhope area into the 1990s, mainly for fluorspar.

There are still many reminders of Rookhope's industrial past in the area – and the most expressive is the great arch near the start of the walk. It is the only surviving fragment of a row of six such arches that carried the 2-mile (3.2km) flue, known as Rookhope Chimney, from the smelt works at Lintzgarth across the valley. After crossing the river, the flue ran for 1 mile (1.6km) underground and ½ mile (800m) up the hillside. Its purpose was to cool the gases from the smelting floor, in which there was much vaporised lead. The lead was deposited on the walls of the flue, and was either scraped off or washed away with water flowing along the tunnel into special 'fume tanks'. The car park is the site of one of them.

The Rookhope area's mining relics were a formative influence on the poet W H Auden (1907–73). Lead mining fascinated Auden as a boy, and a visit he made to Rookhope in

1919, when he was 12, proved a life-changing experience. He suddenly saw these derelict remains as symbols of mankind's lost beliefs. His poems of the 1920s contain many references to the industry, including technical terms that must have puzzled many of his readers. Auden himself was in no doubt of the importance of his Rookhope experience 'There in Rookhope,' he wrote in *New Year Letter*, 'I was first aware of self and not-self, Death and Dread.'

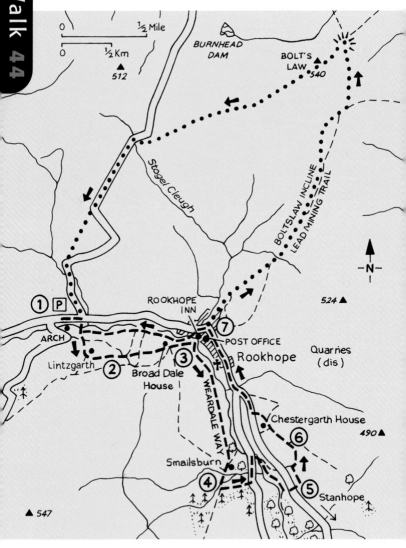

Walk 44 **Directions**

① Walk towards **Rookhope**. Opposite the Blanchland road go right, over a stile and footbridge.

Go ahead, bending left when past the white building, then right on to a track. Go through a gate, and left, uphill. After a cattle grid bear left when the track divides. Go through two metal gates to a white house.

② Just beyond, take a path left then descend and go through a gate in the wall on your right. Cross the field to a stile, then on through a gate towards a stile by farm buildings. Pass in front of them to a wooden stile. Head downhill towards the village, to a ladder stile.

WHERE TO EAT AND DRINK
In Rookhope the **Rose and Crown** near the church offers meals and real ale (dogs allowed). The **Rookhope Inn** also has real ale, and home-cooked food. Both provide a pleasant place to stop and children are welcome, but check at the Rose and Crown when you arrive.

③ After the stile walk past buildings and turn right along the track for ¾ mile (1.2km), going through three gates, then through a farmyard with two more. Follow the track beyond, uphill, to where it bends left.

④ Turn left. As the track disappears continue downhill to a stile. Turn left along the road. Just after a small lay-by go right over a stile, signed 'Weardale Way'. Cross the footbridge and climb the path opposite, bearing right. Walk through the field, go over a stile then uphill to a gate on the ridge.

⑤ Cross the lane and go through a gate opposite. The track curves left then disappears. Go towards the left of the buildings, then bear left

keeping beside the wall. At the field end go right, over a stile, then head left to a gate by the house.

⑥ Go through the gate and up steps on your right to a hand gate into the field. Turn left, behind the house, go though a gate and cross the field bearing slightly left to another gate. Walk behind the buildings and at the end take a wooden gate to the left of a metal farm gate. Pass the large farm building then go downhill to a stile on to a lane. Turn right, then right again at the junction into **Rookhope** village.

WHILE YOU'RE THERE
Visit nearby **Stanhope**, called the Capital of Weardale. In the churchyard is the fossilised stump of a 250 million-year-old tree. In Heathery Burn Cave near by, the possessions of a Bronze-Age family (now in the British Museum) were discovered in 1850. For today's visitors there is an open-air swimming pool and pleasant walks beside the River Wear.

⑦ Pass the post office and the **Rookhope Inn**, then take a signed path, left. Cross the bridge and turn right along the track at the 'Rookhope Trails' sign. The path ascends to a higher track. Continue over a stile and ahead, past the nursery. After a gate and a wooden stile, turn right over the footbridge, go over the stile and turn left on the road back to the start.

WHAT TO LOOK FOR
From Rookhope to Smailsburn farm the walk follows the route of the former **railway line** built by the Weardale Coal and Iron Company. The route continues beyond Smailsburn for another 3 miles (4.8km) to Westgate where it originally joined the Wear Valley line. According to a late 19th-century survey, the line was 'used for the conveyance of coal, limestone, lead, &c. Coal for the village, smelt-mill, and Westgate; limestone from the quarry of the Weardale Coal and Iron Company to their iron-works, and lead from the mines to the smelt-mill, and thence to the market.' The mines and quarries around the Rookhope Burn valley also had their own branches, some of them of smaller gauge.

Consett Steel and the River Derwent

Along the banks of the river which first brought steel making to Consett.

•DISTANCE•	3½ miles (5.7km)
•MINIMUM TIME•	1hr 30min
•ASCENT / GRADIENT•	311ft (95m) ▲ ▲ ▲
•LEVEL OF DIFFICULTY•	🚶🚶 🚶🚶 🚶🚶
•PATHS•	River and streamside paths with some roadside walking
•LANDSCAPE•	Pastoral landscapes with reminders of industrial past
•SUGGESTED MAP•	aqua3 OS Explorer 307 Consett & Derwent Reservoir
•START / FINISH•	Grid reference: NZ 085518
•DOG FRIENDLINESS•	Can be off lead for most of walk – look for notices
•PARKING•	Car park off Sandy Lane, off A691
•PUBLIC TOILETS•	Allensford Country Park (may be closed in winter)

BACKGROUND TO THE WALK

Even into the late 1970s views of Consett would still be described as 'terrible and magnificent'. As Henry Thorold's *Shell Guide to County Durham*, published in 1980, recorded, 'Vulcan's great forges stand there on the hillside enveloped in steam; cooling towers, cylinders, chimneys, incredible and intimidating.' It was true then – just. But the steel mills of Consett closed in that very year, bringing to an end a story of growth and enterprise that began in 1837 when iron ore was discovered here. The first works opened four years later: by the 1880s the Consett Iron Company, founded in 1864 as a successor to the Derwent Iron Company, employed more than 6,000 people in the rapidly-expanded town. The closure a century later could have devastated Consett. Instead, it has reinvented itself as a place of growing service and manufacturing industry, which also looks back with pride to its history of steel making.

The Derwent Valley

Dividing Northumberland and Durham, this stretch of the River Derwent was the cradle of the northern steel industry. Forge Cottage, just over the footbridge at the start of the walk, indicates that iron working had been long established in the valley. German steel makers, producing fine swords, lived in Shotley Bridge as early as the 1690s – the village later became the fashionable place for the upper middle classes of Consett to live. Shotley Bridge was also a spa – in 1841 it was said that it would soon come to rival Harrogate, Cheltenham and Leamington. As the walk approaches Allensford, there are the remains of a 17th-century ironworks near by.

Allensford Country Park and Woods

Developed by Durham County Council – and right on its northern boundary – Allensford Country Park consists of 14 acres (5.7ha) of riverside grassland. As well as pleasant walks, there are play facilities for children and access for people using wheelchairs. Within the park is Allensford Wood – the walk takes you through part of it. It is semi-natural ancient woodland that is mainly of oak and birch. There has been some recent replanting with native species. A series of trails criss-crosses the wood; the routes are marked with a symbol of a walking man.

Steelworks Site

The section of the walk along Pemberton Road between the road junction (see Point ⑤) and the path into the woodland seems quiet today. But until 1980 the whole of the area to your right, now landscaped and grassed, was one of the most industrialised in the country. Here stood one of the British Steel Corporation's mills, its huge buildings alive with noise, smoke and heat. Today it provides an area for recreation and enjoyment, crossed by paths that follow the old railway lines that served the works.

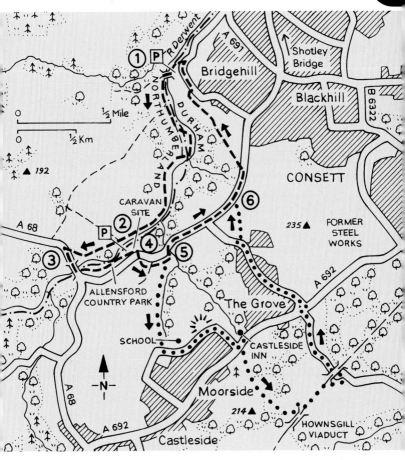

Walk 45 Directions

① From the car park, walk beside the house, following the wall, and bend right to cross the river on a footbridge. Turn left along the river bank and follow it through woodland. Where the path divides stay by the river. Eventually reach an area of beech woodland where the path rises on to a wider track.

Walk 45

② Follow the track, keeping left when it forks – there are waymarks on this section. The path follows a wire fence, and eventually bears right over a tiny stone bridge skirting a house to reach the **A68**.

③ Turn left down the hill. Go over the road bridge, passing from Northumberland into Durham. Where a road joins from the left, go left through the entrance into **Allensford Country Park**. Bear round to the right, and walk through the grassed riverside area to a car park. Go through the car park to reach a road by the entrance to the caravan site.

④ Go ahead across the road to a waymarked stile in a fence opposite. Follow the path, which goes up two sets of steps. At the top follow the grassy path. Where it divides, bear to the left and follow the winding path into woodland and continue downhill. When you reach a crossing path by a marker post, turn left to the road.

⑤ Turn right and follow the road (take care because it can be busy). It rises through woodland and then passes through a more open area. After ½ mile (800m), pass a road off to the right. In ¼ mile (400m) beyond, look for a footpath that descends on your right to meet the road, by trees.

⑥ Continue to follow the road for 400yds (366m). As the roads rises, take a signed footpath left, downhill into woodland. The path opens out into a track, then becomes a path again. Follow the path for ½ mile (800m) to reach a lane. Turn left here, downhill. At the bottom of the hill turn left again, following the car park sign back to the start of the walk.

Derwent Valley's Past

Communism, steel making and Roman remains at Chopwell.

•DISTANCE•	7 miles (11.3km)
•MINIMUM TIME•	2hrs 30min
•ASCENT / GRADIENT•	541ft (165m) ▲ ▲ ▲
•LEVEL OF DIFFICULTY•	🚶🚶 🚶🚶 🚶🚶
•PATHS•	Tracks, field paths and old railway line
•LANDSCAPE•	Woodland and riverside, farmland and industrial remains
•SUGGESTED MAP•	aqua3 OS Explorer 307 Consett & Derwent Reservoir
•START / FINISH•	Grid reference: NZ122579
•DOG FRIENDLINESS•	On lead, except on former railway line
•PARKING•	Roadside parking in Chopwell; follow signs for 'Chopwell Park Car Park'. Car park, itself, opens irregularly
•PUBLIC TOILETS•	None on route

BACKGROUND TO THE WALK

It was coal mining that created the village of Chopwell that we see today, with its red-brick buildings and no-nonsense atmosphere – and it was the miners who earned it the name 'Little Moscow' in the 1920s. The coal won from local mines was predominantly used for making coke to stoke the furnaces of the Consett Iron Company. When coal production declined after World War One, many miners were made redundant or put on short-time working. These conditions allowed Communist sympathisers to assume the running of the village. A miners' strike from July 1925 to December 1926 led to accusations of a Communist takeover of the local Labour Party. A national newspaper declared that 'the village is known far and wide as the reddest in England.' Streets were renamed after Marx, Engels and Lenin, and it is said that there were Communist Sunday schools in the village, as well as 'Das Kapital' on the lectern of the local church. For a time the hammer and sickle flag flew over the town hall.

The Cradle of Steel

The area between Blackhall Mill and Derwentcote Ironworks was once the centre of the steel industry in Britain. Steel was made here initially to supply the sword manufacturers of Shotley Bridge, eastwards along the river. Derwentcote, the earliest steel-making furnace to have survived, was built around 1720 and worked until the 1870s. Another furnace at Blackhall Mill lasted until 1834, when a flood washed away its mill dam; the mill was demolished at the beginning of the 20th century. Derwentcote survived, and is now cared for by English Heritage. It is open summer weekends, and contains an interesting explanatory display.

Along the Line

Beyond Derwentcote the walk enters Byerside Wood and then joins the old railway line that now forms the 12½-mile (20.1km) footpath and cycle route of the Derwent Valley Country Park. The route runs from Consett to Gateshead and, at its western end, connects with other

Walk 46

former railway routes, including the Waskerley Way and the Consett and Sunderland Railway Path.

In contrast to the industrial theme of much of the walk, the history of Ebchester stretches much further back in time. Here was the site of the Roman fort of Vindomara, strategically placed where the road we know as Dere Street, which ran from York to the Firth of Forth, crossed the Derwent. Constructed around AD 80, the original timber buildings were later replaced by stone and the fort was finally abandoned in 410. A signboard by the post office shows the layout. It is possible to see its ramparts north of the main road and in the village churchyard. There is a Roman altar in the church tower.

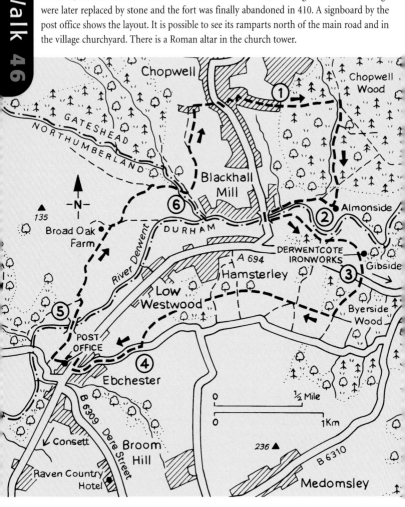

Walk 46 **Directions**

① Walk up the entrance road to **Chopwell Park**. Turn right past a metal barrier and bear right, past the 'Chopwell Woodland Park' sign. Follow the woodland track, turning right at a crossing track. Pass another barrier to a metalled area. Turn right and follow the track downhill. Where the woodland ends go over a stile and continue down a fenced path. Enter **Almonside** farmyard through a gate.

② Bear right and follow the track to the road in **Blackhall Mill**. Turn left, over the bridge. Just after a footpath sign, go left along a field edge, right of the hedge. Follow the fenced riverside path. At a crossing path, turn left, uphill. At the top go sharp left, following waymark signs. Go left of the buildings, over a stile and across the field. Go over two wooden stiles then right. Follow the track uphill, passing **Derwentcote Ironworks**, to the main road.

Walk 46

WHILE YOU'RE THERE

The National Trust's **Gibside Estate** is 4 miles (6.4km) east of Chopwell. Once home to the Bowes-Lyon family, the estate has riverside and forest walks, and a number of ornate buildings, including an 18th-century chapel and 140ft (42.5m) Column of British Liberty. The Gothic Banqueting House is now a holiday cottage.

WHERE TO EAT AND DRINK

In the centre of Chopwell and in Blackhall Mill there are several pubs that serve food. A little up the hill from where the former railway line joins the lane into Ebchester is the **Raven Country Hotel**, which offers both bar meals and a restaurant; children welcome.

---

③ Cross and take a signed footpath almost opposite. Go over a stile and, at a crossing path, turn right to another stile. Follow the path through woodland to the former railway track. Turn right and follow the track, which crosses another track (barriers at each side) and eventually rises to another barrier on to a metalled lane.

④ Turn right and descend into **Ebchester.** Bend right by the community centre to meet the main road. Cross over and turn right in front of the **post office**. Turn left at the footpath sign beyond. Follow the fence on your left, bend left at

the end beside the wall, then follow the footpath downhill to reach a metalled lane. Turn right along the lane to a footbridge.

⑤ Cross the bridge. The footpath bends right before going straight ahead across the field to a stile. Follow the green lane uphill, pass a farmhouse and follow the track through two gates. Where the main track bears left, go straight ahead. Go through a farm gate, and along the field edge. Go though two gates to a T-junction of tracks.

⑥ Turn left, signposted 'Whinney Leas'. About 300yds (274m) after the farm go right, over a stile, and walk across the field to another stile, hidden in a hedge. Continue up the field to another stile right of the houses, and along a narrow lane. At the end, turn right along the tarmac lane. At the main road turn right and then left, following 'Chopwell Park Car Park' signs back to your car.

WHAT TO LOOK FOR

The 949-acre (384ha) **Chopwell Wood** was once a wild area of oaks and hazel. Much affected by coal mining in the 19th and early 20th centuries, when a railway ran through it, it was taken over by the Forestry Commission in 1919, and largely felled during the two world wars. Restocking from 1952 has left it a mainly coniferous forest, with larch, pine and spruce. There are still patches of earlier broadleaved woodland remaining, however, some of it coppiced. The wood, which became a Woodland Park in 1994 and is managed by Forest Enterprise with the help of a local group, provides habitats for a wide variety of animals, including red squirrels, bats and, in the pools formed in three World War Two bomb craters, great crested newts.

Valley of the Shining Water

Exploring one of Northumberland's most attractive river valleys.

•DISTANCE•	3¾ miles (6km)
•MINIMUM TIME•	2hrs 15min
•ASCENT / GRADIENT•	590ft (180m) ▲ ▲ ▲
•LEVEL OF DIFFICULTY•	🚶 🚶 🚶
•PATHS•	Good river paths and faint field paths, 19 stiles
•LANDSCAPE•	Riverside and high pasture
•SUGGESTED MAP•	aqua3 OS Explorer OL43 Hadrian's Wall
•START / FINISH•	Grid reference: NY 838558
•DOG FRIENDLINESS•	Farming country, keep dogs on leads
•PARKING•	Ample parking in village centre
•PUBLIC TOILETS•	In village centre

BACKGROUND TO THE WALK

If you were dropped into East Allendale you could be forgiven for thinking you were in the northern part of the Yorkshire Dales. Like that area it's rugged rather than beautiful, but it's also peaceful and serene. Appropriately, Allen comes from the Celtic word 'aln' which means shining or foaming. The main centre, Allendale Town, is set on a hillside overlooking a bend in the East Allen River and sheltered beneath the heather moors of Hexhamshire Common. It proclaims itself to be the true geographical centre of Britain, and co-ordinates inscribed on to the church tower's sundial reinforce this.

Mining Town

On entering the large Market Square with its many large hotels and inns, it soon becomes obvious that this place has seen busier times, and so it has. This was a mining town, the most prosperous in the whole of the region, with good veins of lead and silver. In the halcyon days of the 18th century Allendale had a population of over 5,500, four times what it is today. Allendale was lively, for the miners were hard-working, hard-drinking men who filled each and everyone of the inns. Even with the death of their industry at the turn of the century, the place stayed busy, with motor coaches bringing people from the industrial north east for health and enjoyment.

Perhaps Allendale is most famous for its Baal Fire Festival, which takes place each New Year's Eve. It's said to be of Viking origin. At 11:30PM the pubs empty and a crowd gathers in the square. Suddenly the night sky is lit up by a procession of 40 men dressed in fancy costumes and with flaming tar barrels on their heads. The men, known as guisers, parade around the town streets accompanied by the Allendale Silver Band. Close to midnight the guisers hurl the burning contents of the barrels on to a bonfire, whose flames then explode high into the sky. It's a dangerous procedure, usually resulting in a few singed eyebrows. The church bells chime in the New Year and everybody sings *Auld Lang Syne* before returning to the pub for more celebrations.

There are many long walks from Allendale Town to the moors but a good introduction explores the immediate environs of the valley itself. Passing the old inns you go down to the river, which is lined by fine stands of trees. In spring and early summer the fields and woods will be full of wild flowers like bloody cranesbill, wild primrose, herb Robert and ragwort.

Later the walk climbs away, to high fields and old farms looking down on the rooftops of Allendale Town. The river, in some places hidden by trees, but in others shining among the valley meadows, meanders into the distance to those dark North Pennine moors that yawn across the western skies.

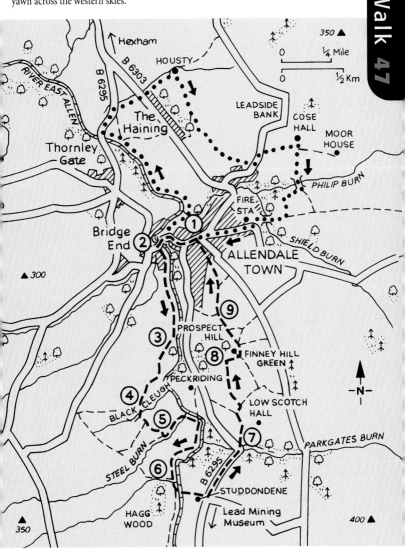

Walk 47 Directions

① From the **Market Place** take the Whitfield road down past the **Hare and Hounds** and round the left-

hand bend to the old **Mill Bridge** across the **River East Allen**.

② Immediately beyond the bridge, turn left along a tarred lane past some cottages – it's highlighted by a

Walk 47

footpath sign 'to Wooley Scar'. Where the track swings right leave it and go through the gate ahead before following a cross-field path, parallel to the river.

③ At the narrow end of a wedge shaped field go over a ladder stile on the right. Here the path veers away from the river and enters an area above **Wooley Scar**, which can be slightly overgrown with nettles and ragwort in the summer months. The route continues generally south west across fields.

④ Beyond **Black Cleugh** it swings south east along a short section of rutted track. Ignoring the first stile on the right follow the right field edge. A waymark on a broken fence points the way down towards the woods surrounding **Steel Burn**.

⑤ Turn left along a grass track running parallel to the burn and go through a gate behind a little cottage. Turn right over a footbridge crossing the burn, then follow the banks of the **East Allen**.

The clear route crosses riverside meadows and ignores the first river footbridge near **Peckriding**.

⑥ After meandering with the river, the path comes upon a track near **Hagg Wood** and follows it across a bridge over the East Allen. The track zig-zags past the farm at **Studdondene** to reach the **B6295** where you turn left.

⑦ On reaching the woods of **Parkgates Burn** take the left of two waymarked paths. Over a stile it climbs fields towards the left of two farmhouses on the skyline – **Low Scotch Hall**. It turns right then left to round the farmhouse, now following the left field edge high above the valley.

⑧ On reaching the woods of **Prospect Hill** turn right through some animal pens then along an enclosed path to the farm of **Finney Hill Green**. Turn left beyond the house and continue along the left edge of three fields.

⑨ A modern housing estate at the edge of **Allendale Town** comes into view and the path heads north, parallel to the houses. In the last field it descends towards some more mature housing and enters an estate through a little ginnel. Go past the children's playground and out on to the main road in the village centre.

Wanlockhead: Scotland's Highest Village

Discover the secrets of lead and gold mining in 'God's Treasure House'.

•DISTANCE•	3¾ miles (6km)
•MINIMUM TIME•	3hrs
•ASCENT / GRADIENT•	525ft (160m) ▲▲ ▲
•LEVEL OF DIFFICULTY•	🚶🚶 🚶🚶 🚶
•PATHS•	Footpaths, hill tracks, hillside and old railway lines, 1 stile
•LANDSCAPE•	Hills, mining relics and village
•SUGGESTED MAP•	aqua3 OS Explorer 329 Lowther Hills, Sanquhar & Leadhills
•START / FINISH•	Grid reference: NX 873129
•DOG FRIENDLINESS•	Keep on lead near livestock
•PARKING•	Museum of Lead Mining car park
•PUBLIC TOILETS•	At car park

BACKGROUND TO THE WALK

A unique combination of changing pressures within the earth's crust several million years ago, led to the formation of rich mineral veins in this part of the Southern Uplands. Everything from gold to zinc and copper has been found locally, but it was the rich deposits of lead that resulted in the establishment of Scotland's highest village. By the 17th century a permanent, if primitive, settlement was established. Accommodation consisted of one-room cottages with often as many as eight people living in them. They cooked over the open fire in the middle of the room and smoke was vented through a hole in the roof.

By the late 19th century, when lead mining was at its peak, some 850 people lived here in much improved cottages. These cottages were bigger, with an attic room and a proper cooking range. In 1871 the miners founded a co-operative society, bought all their supplies there and received a share of the profits. Amazingly this continued until 1971.

A Thriving Community

The miners valued the little leisure time they had and were very active in forming local clubs and societies. There were curling, bowling and quoiting clubs, a drama group and even a silver band. The Library, the second oldest subscription library in Europe, was founded in 1756 by the minister and a small group of villagers. Wanlockhead fared better than most libraries with a donation of books from the local landowner the Duke of Buccleuch. Buccleuch also allowed the miners the use of land to keep cattle and grow vegetables and, in 1842, he funded the building of a new school and the salary of the teacher.

The miners' children learned to read, write and count and could also take lessons in Latin and Greek. A government inspector visiting in 1842 was so impressed by the standard of learning he concluded that '…the children of the poor labourers of Wanlockhead are under as good, or perhaps better system of intellectual culture than even the middle class children of South Britain generally.'

As the price of lead slumped, and mines became exhausted, the miners gradually drifted away. The last of the mines, Glencrieff, closed in 1934 and the village went into decline until only 30 people remained. In the 1960s the local authority offered to re-house them elsewhere but they resolutely refused to leave. Thanks to their determination, an influx of new blood, renovation of houses and the opening of the Museum of Lead Mining, Wanlockhead has survived as a community into the 21st century. But it almost vanished, like countless other mining villages, which are now just names on the map, a few ruins, fading memories, old photographs and tales.

Walk 48 **Directions**

① With the **museum** to your back turn left and join the **Southern Upland Way**. Head uphill on steps

then, at the top, cross to a stone building with a large white door. Turn right on to a rough road, cross the main road and take the public footpath to **Enterkine Pass**. Follow this to the front of a white house.

Walk 48

② Turn left on to an old railway. Follow this, cross a road then go through a long cutting to reach a fence. Go over a stile to **Glengonnar Station** then follow the narrow path that runs along the left side of the railway tracks from here.

③ Eventually the path runs on to a rough road and in the distance you will see two terraced houses. At the point where the telephone wires intersect the road turn left at the pole on the left-hand side and follow the line of the fence down to some sheep pens. Turn right at the end of the pens and walk out to the main road.

WHERE TO EAT AND DRINK   ⓘ

The **café/tea room** attached to the museum is geared towards families and has a splendid menu of light meals, sandwiches, snacks and delicious hot soup. It's a light and airy place conveniently situated where the walk begins and ends. Occasionally in the summer local musicians play traditional music here.

---

④ Turn right then almost immediately left on to a hill road. Walk uphill on this until the road bears sharp right and a dirt track forks off to the left. Turn left on to the track and keep on it until you reach a gate. Cross over then veer left on to a faint track. Follow the track downhill to the point where it comes close to the corner of a fence on your left.

⑤ Cross the fence and go straight ahead on a very faint track picking your way through the heather. Eventually, as the track begins to look more like a recognisable path, you will reach a fork. Go to the right here and cross the flank of the hill passing through some disused tips.

⑥ The path at this point is little more than a series of sheep tracks and may disappear altogether but that is not a problem. Ahead of you is a large conical spoil heap and, provided you keep heading towards it, you know you will be going in the right direction.

⑦ Towards the end of the hill the track heads left, starts to make its way downhill, then passes behind a row of cottages. Veer right, downhill, after the cottages to join the road. Turn left and continue past **Glencrieff cottages** then turn right, leaving the road and heading downhill again. Cross a bridge and climb up on to the **Southern Upland Way**. Turn left along it and follow this route back to the car park.

WHAT TO LOOK FOR   ⓘ

The Wanlockhead **beam engine** was used in the 19th century to drain the Straitsteps mine. It worked by using an ingenious arrangement that filled a bucket at one end with water, thus pulling the beam end down and lifting the piston at the other end to expel the water from the mine.

WHILE YOU'RE THERE   ⓘ

A visit to the **Museum of Lead Mining** before you start will greatly enhance your understanding of the area and your enjoyment of the walk. The entire history of gold and lead mining in this area is covered and the admission fee includes a visit to a former miners' cottage and a trip into one of the mines (wear warm clothing). During the summer there are gold panning demonstrations and courses. The museum is open from April to October, daily.

Discover Dunaskin Iron Works

A hill walk from a 19th-century industrial monument to a deserted, but not forgotten, village.

•DISTANCE•	4 miles (6.4km)
•MINIMUM TIME•	3hrs
•ASCENT / GRADIENT•	492ft (150m) ▲ ▲ ▲
•LEVEL OF DIFFICULTY•	🚶🚶 🚶🚶 🚶🚶
•PATHS•	Old rail and tram beds and rough hillside
•LANDSCAPE•	Hill, moorland and industrial buildings
•SUGGESTED MAP•	aqua3 OS Explorer 327 Cumnock & Dalmellington
•START / FINISH•	Grid reference: NX 440084
•DOG FRIENDLINESS•	Keep on lead near sheep and at lambing time
•PARKING•	Dunaskin Open Air Museum
•PUBLIC TOILETS•	At visitor centre

BACKGROUND TO THE WALK

During the Industrial Revolution, iron was one of the great growth industries. In 1836 Henry Houldsworth, owner of a mill in Glasgow, diversified his business interests and created the Coltness Iron Works. Ten years later he and his son John brought the iron industry to the remote Doon Valley. Henry built his iron foundry on the site of Dunaskin farm and the early Victorian field pattern remains in outline surrounding the works.

New Industry

The area, although rich in iron, coal and water, was almost totally lacking in transport links. Everything for the construction of the foundry had to be brought in by train to Ayr and then by horse to Dunaskin. Twenty four pairs of horses were needed to haul the great beam for the blast engines alone. Iron was continually produced here from 1848 until 1921, when the buildings became a brickworks and then a processing plant for the coal mines until the late 1970s. One of the most complete Industrial Revolution ironworks in Europe, it has now been restored by a conservation trust and is open as a museum.

At the time the Dunaskin Iron Works were built, the principal industries of the area were agriculture and weaving and the population of the Upper Doon Valley was a mere 250 at Patna and a further 800 in the parish of Dalmellington. Skilled workers were brought in to provide the core of the workforce for the ironworks. They were joined by local men, leaving agricultural work in hope of higher wages, as well as tin miners from Cornwall, itinerant English workers and Highlanders displaced by the Clearances.

New Homes

The company built Waterside village opposite the ironworks to house the workers. High above on the Knockkippen plateau, twin villages were built close to the iron ore mines. The two villages of Lethanhill and Burnfoothill were considered as one, commonly known as the 'Hill, by the close-knit communities. Linked to the outside world by tram and railway lines this community survived the closure of the mines, the end of smelting at Dunaskin and two world wars. Ironically it was killed off by the post-war drive to improve housing.

Sanitation and overcrowding were a problem on the 'Hill and when the local authority decided to concentrate new building in nearby Patna and Dalmellington, the quality of the new housing was irresistible. No one wanted to leave but gradually the population dwindled until the last man, James Stevenson, departed on 31 August 1954. All that remains today are the bare outlines of houses among the trees, the war memorial with its poppy wreath still laid each Armistice Sunday and a simple stone painted white with the poignant inscription 'Long live the 'Hill 1851–1954'.

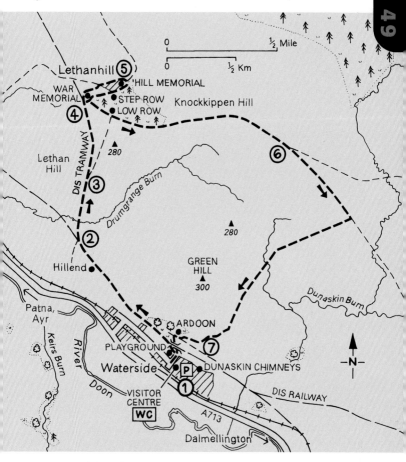

Walk 49 Directions

① Turn right in front of the **visitor centre** and follow the road towards the adventure playground. Go uphill on a track to the right of the playground and through woodland. Emerge at a T-junction opposite a **railway bridge** and turn left on to a grassy trail.

② When you reach a metal gate across the trail, go through a small wooden one at its side. Climb over the next gate, turn right and head uphill following the line of a disused tramway, between the ends

Walk 49

of an old bridge. This is the trackbed of the former horse-drawn tramway, which was used to bring the iron ore down from the plateau.

③ At the top of the hill, when the path divides, keep left and follow the path as it goes through two short sections of wall. The ground to your right in front of the conifer plantation was once the village football field. Where the path is blocked by a fence, turn right, then go left through a gate and right on to a metalled lane.

WHAT TO LOOK FOR
The foundations of the former church and schoolhouse can be seen on the ground behind the war memorial. The church was sold to a local silver band and was rebuilt in Dalmellington. Look also in the remains of the houses of **Low Row** for floral tributes hung on the trees by former residents who still walk here on a regular basis.

④ Head along here, past the remains of the miners' houses of **Step Row**, which are clearly visible amongst the trees. A stone **memorial** to the 'Hill stands near the site of the former village store. To the right of this, and now within the wood, is the former village square and the remains of more houses.

⑤ From the stone memorial turn back towards the war memorial, then return to the gate at the corner of the wood and continue along the

WHERE TO EAT AND DRINK
The child-friendly **Chimneys Restaurant**, which is part of the Dunaskin Open Air Museum, is a fairly basic sort of place but the friendly staff serve up a decent variety of good quality food and an excellent bowl of soup which is just the job on a cold day. When Chimneys is closed try one of the hotels in the centre of Dalmellington.

track beside the wood. In the trees are the remains of **Low Row**. Go Through another gate and continue along the former railway. When it forks, keep right.

⑥ Continue until the route ahead is blocked by sheets of corrugated iron, near a wall. Turn right and follow the line of the wall downhill. Cross a wall and continue walking downhill towards the chimneys of Dunaskin. When you reach a broken hedge, near the end of the **Green Hill**, turn right along the front of it and continue along here until you are level with the second of Dunaskin's chimneys.

⑦ Turn left here, heading downhill a short way and then though a gate. Veer to the right and head towards a wooded area. Go through the wood and emerge at **Ardoon**. Go past the house, turn left on to a footpath and follow it downhill and under a small, disused railway bridge. Cross the track and carry on heading back downhill on the footpath which leads back to the visitor centre.

WHILE YOU'RE THERE
Naturally a visit to the **Dunaskin Open Air Museum** should not be missed, it is open April–October, daily 10–5. Allow at least 2 hours for a visit and wear sturdy footwear and outdoor clothing. Just along the road, on the north edge of Dallmellington, is the **Scottish Industrial Railway Centre**, operated by enthusiasts from the Ayrshire Rail Preservation Group. This is as much part of the local story as the ironworks and every Sunday in July and August they offer trips on a working steam train.

On Old Roads and Rails Around Muirkirk

Walk around a once prosperous moorland town that stood at the crossroads of history.

•DISTANCE•	3½ miles (5.7km)
•MINIMUM TIME•	3hrs
•ASCENT / GRADIENT•	16ft (5m) ▲ ▲ ▲
•LEVEL OF DIFFICULTY•	🚶 🚶 🚶
•PATHS•	Old railway beds, farm tracks and country lanes, 1 stile
•LANDSCAPE•	Moorland, pastures and woodland
•SUGGESTED MAP•	aqua3 OS Explorer 328 Sanquhar & New Cumnock
•START / FINISH•	Grid reference: NX 696265
•DOG FRIENDLINESS•	Good, locals walk their dogs here
•PARKING•	Walkers' car park, Furnace Road
•PUBLIC TOILETS•	None on route

BACKGROUND TO THE WALK

In the early 17th century Muirkirk was little more than a crude little settlement called Garan on a dirt track that ran from Ayr to Edinburgh. The building of the Moor Kirk of Kyle led eventually to a name change to Muirkirk. An abundance of minerals such as coal, limestone and iron ore in the locality would inevitably make it a centre of industry and bring great prosperity.

'Tar' McAdam
Coal mining was well under way when John Loudon McAdam (1756–1836) came here in 1786 to set up a tar works. Known locally as 'Tar' McAdam, he would later go on to develop his famous method of road construction and this is where he carried out his first experiments. Furnace Road leading to the walkers' car park was used in his first trials and road surfaces are still referred to as tarmac today.

Iron and Coal
Muirkirk became the site of Ayrshire's first ironworks in 1787 when James Ewing & Co opened here. Three years later a canal had been dug to transport ore and coal on a series of barges from the Lightshaw, Auldhouseburn and Crossflat mines east of the works. Tram lines ran to the west and a series of bogie tracks led from the various pits to the canals. The Kames Colliery was opened in 1799 and would become the longest operating coal mine in the area. The canal was eventually replaced by the railway when the Glasgow and South Western Railway Company opened the Auckinleck-to-Muirkirk branch line in 1848. From this main line a maze of spur lines ran to the production areas.

Muirkirk had become a prosperous and thriving community. It was the first town in Britain to get gas lighting following the construction of the Muirkirk Coke & Gaslight Co in 1859. At its peak, the town had a population in excess of 5,000 with 1,000 employed in the ironworks alone.

Into Decline

But nothing lasts forever. Mines become exhausted, or seams run out and industrial trends change. The ironworks ceased production in 1923, following a strike by the workers. Iron ore mining had stopped some time previously and the ore was shipped in from further afield. During the strike the furnaces cooled with iron still inside them and rather than go to the expense of restoring them the company shut down.

The elaborate façade of the works which locals had dubbed 'The Castle' was demolished in 1968, the same year that the Kames Colliery finally closed. By this time the railway had disappeared under the axe of Dr Beeching in the mid-1960s. With no industry left the population drifted away and Muirkirk gradually declined to the small community that remains today.

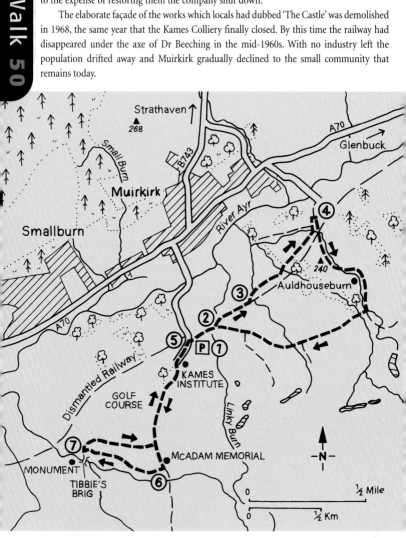

Walk 50 **Directions**

① From the car park follow the blue waymarker and exit via a gate on to a rough track with a high wall running along to the right. This continues as a fence and, once past the end of it, look for a waymarker pole on the left.

② Turn left on to a grass track. Follow this to some steps, go downhill and through a kissing

Walk 50

gate. Turn right and walk along what may have been the bank of the 18th-century canal. Go through a kissing gate then veer left on to a rough track at the next waymarker.

③ Follow this to a duckboard and stile, cross here, turn left on to a short section of gravel path then turn right at a waymarker. The railway track here appears to fork. Keep to the left and continue along the trackbed eventually reaching a kissing gate.

④ Go through the gate and turn right on to the quiet country road. Follow this past the remains of an old railway bridge, past a farm entrance on the right then go through a gate to continue on a farm road. At the next gate turn right, go through four gates and return to the car park.

⑤ Turn right and exit the car park on to **Furnace Road** then turn left. Continue past the clock tower of the derelict **Kames Institute** and along the edge of a golf course. Go through a gate and continue, passing a cottage on the left, on to the old drove road to Sanquhar. Go through another gate and continue to the **McAdam memorial**.

⑥ Just past this head along a green track on the right. When it forks left on to what may have been a

tramline keep right. Follow this track along the side of a stream until it joins a dirt track just above **Tibbie's Brig**. Near here, in a small clay dwelling lived a local poetess, Tibbie Pagan, who eked out a living by singing, selling her poetry and possibly supplying illicit whisky. She is believed locally to have been the source of the song *Ca the Yowes tae the Knowes* although Burns himself collected it from a clergyman. She published a volume of her poems in 1803.

⑦ Go down to the **Brig** and the monument then return uphill keeping left on the access for the disabled route to McAdam's cairn. Follow this back to the drove road where you turn left to return to the car park.

Acknowledgements

Front cover: View of Ironbridge town from Iron Bridge, AA World Travel Library/M Hayward